WHO IS LIKE THE LORD?

MEKHI'S STORY

As told by

SIMPLY NICOLE

COPYRIGHT

Who Is Like the Lord?

IBSN- 978-0-578-59353-1

©2019 by Simply Nicole

Published by

Simply Nicole Publishing

Washington, DC

Printed in the United States of America.

This book or parts thereof may not be reproduced in any form, stored in a retrieval system, or transmitted in any form by any means – electronic, mechanical, photocopy, recording or otherwise – without prior written permission of the publisher, except as provided by the United States of America copyright law.

This book is available at special quantity discounts for bulk purchase for sales promotions, fund- raising and educational needs. For information please write the author at Simplynicolebooks@gmail.com or Authorsimplynicole@gmail.com

You can also follow the author on Instagram at Simply_nicolepublishing and on Twitter at SimplynicoleIam

This book is a memoir. It reflects the author's past and present recollections of experiences over time. Some names and characteristics have been changed, some events have been compressed, and/or left out for legal reasons, and some dialogue has been recreated.

DEDICATION

I would like to dedicate this book to my angel who awaits me in another lifetime. I would also like to dedicate this book to everyone that said I would not amount to anything. To everyone that counted me out, judged and made me feel less than for being different. Hopefully your souls find eternal peace. The potter wants to use you again. There's an artist waiting to be discovered in us all. Keep chiseling until that masterpiece is discovered.

~Ase~

ACKKOWLEDGMENTS

First and foremost, I would like to give th(ankhs) to the Creator. I finally understand my purpose. Th(ankh) you for seeing me fit for this assignment.

To my mother and father, th(ankh) you for instilling in me that I can do anything I put my mind to. It meant the world to me to have your support during this storm.

In the words of Snoop Dogg,

"I want to thank me

I want to thank me for believing in me

I want to thank me for doing all this hard work.

I want to thank me for having no days off

I want to thank me for never quitting

I want to thank me for always being a giver and trying to give more than I receive.

I want to thank me for trying to do more right than wrong.

I want to thank me, for just being me at all times."

~Uncle Snoop~

I would like to recognize all the family and friends that came to see my son.

My mother Margaret, My father Andrew, My sisters Jennifer and Kyerrial

Brothers Jonah and Karim, Aunts Lynette and Shalonda, Uncle Boo

I would like to recognize Facebook. Without that platform, this book would be impossible.

If I forgot to mention your name, please charge it to my head and not my heart.

To my cousin Misha whom I just met last year in an unfortunate event, Th(Ankh) you for offering me healing. May your light forever shine.

All Praises due to the most high.

MEKHI'S STORY

MEKHI'S STORY

When the dust settled, a childless mother, found herself carrying the burdens of memories and mistakes. I had been saying that I wanted to write a book detailing the short life and tragic death of an angel that I had the pleasure of birthing. He lived twenty-seven short days, so I thought I would highlight and reflect on every day of life in each chapter. I would finish by bringing awareness to the disease that claimed the life of my young soldier. A disease I had never heard of – Necrotizing Enterocolitis Totalis. I would also speak on the importance of a healthy pregnancy, the importance of not smoking/ drinking, and avoiding domestic violence at all costs. Parents are not supposed to bury their children. He should be here giving his other brothers a tough time. However, he is not! Nothing but bittersweet memories remains. I feel robbed. I yearn for an understanding. What good is closure when it will never bring back what was lost? Can you still be called a mother when your child is no longer here, and your actions and non-actions are the reason they are gone? In this book, I will reveal intimate details that will give the reader an understanding as to why things went the way they did and why Mekhi had to go. Since his death I have gone through periods of darkness and self-destruction. I do blame myself so quite naturally I struggle with guilt and depression. I cannot help but wonder if my Peanut blames me for his death as much as I do and if he could forgive me. How does someone beg for forgiveness over a situation that was self-inflicted? The saying is so cliché, but if I had known then what I know now, I would have done things differently. I WOULD HAVE, I SWEAR I WOULD HAVE! The only thing that brings me peace is writing all my memories of my son. One lesson to take from this tragedy; when God is trying to get your attention, he will use and remove loved ones to get it. He had to die so that I may live. Process that!

Introduction

  May 14, 2015, I went to the emergency room after experiencing a rash on my thighs, vaginal bleeding and a discharge. A routine urine test confirmed my suspicions of being pregnant. I mean after all my last menstrual period was April 17, 2015. I was not too concerned about the rash. I figured it was a reaction from the chlorine at a hotel pool. My first response to learning of my pregnancy was the common excitement and joy that I think all moms experience. Deep inside I am scared because I was a single mother of six other children living in a transitional shelter. When did I find the time to get pregnant? That hotel experience that left me with a sexually transmitted infection afterwards, that is when! Ladies when you lie down with dogs be prepared to wake up with fleas. They say God does not give you any more than you can bear. Someone please find the "they" and bring "them" to me so I can punch "them and they" in the face. That statement is so far from the truth.

  After a physical altercation with the father of the babies; I had returned to the emergency room on Sunday May 31, 2015, with an eye that would remain closed for a week and vaginal bleeding. I urge any and everyone who deals with domestic violence just to feel halfway loved and wanted to get out. Break that chain and free yourself from that psychological torture and mental bondage. You cannot change a man unless he is wearing diapers. PERIOD! The sonogram had revealed the start of my horror. I had been diagnosed with a sub chorionic hemorrhage. In other words, the bigger the babies grew, the more they would detach themselves from the placenta. Doctors told me not to worry about prenatal care because with all the bleeding that had been taking place it would be a matter of time before I miscarry. On that day, I was six weeks and three days pregnant. Three weeks had passed, and to everyone's surprise, I was still pregnant. I eagerly scheduled my prenatal visit for a date in July.

On July 17, 2015, the caseworker at the shelter I was living at had called me to let me know she was transferring me to another building. I had to do all the moving myself and that started the bleeding again. I went back to the hospital where it was confirmed that a miscarriage had taken place. I cried, I screamed and shouted. Lord please make it stop. After having a sonogram done and seeing the remaining baby fighting for life, I vowed to stay away from anything or anyone that could bring us harm. This Angel was determined to grace me with his presence, and I was determined to help him. I had my prenatal appointment. Peanut was growing well. My due date was set for January 22, 2016. I thought we had made it out of the dark. I was wrong. The sex of the baby had been confirmed on September 3, 2015 at an appointment to check on the anatomy and growth. Another baby boy. The lucky number seven. I wanted to name him Lucky. He was growing good at nineteen weeks and six days.

MEKHI'S STORY

I went on to schedule the next three appointments. They were for October 6, 2015, November 27, 2015 (I knew you would be a plump turkey after thanksgiving) and December 28, 2015. Something went wrong and on September 15, 2015, I went to the hospital with contractions in my lower back, and what I thought to be leaking amniotic fluid. I had been rushed through because it was close to shift change. I had been in and out within twenty minutes. That was hardly any time for a proper evaluation and observation. The doctor came back with a determination that I had urinated myself and I was discharged. This went on for a week. Time would go on to reveal just how unlucky my son was. On September 23, 2015, I remember driving my sister to a tattoo shop. I could barely sit up straight; I was in so much pain. I had gone into active labor sometime between September 15-23, 2015. I ignored all the warning signs of having an early baby because I just knew I could never give birth prematurely.

My other children were all full term. I ignored the pain because I have a high tolerance for pain. I minimized labor for normal stomach aches. Maybe it was something I had to eat. I had taken all the pain I could take and had my sister drive me to Washington Hospital Center. I knew I was in labor. A sonogram was performed and after looking at the horror on the screen my mouth dropped along with my sisters' mouth. There was no fluid around my baby. NONE! Not even one drop! Drugs were given to me to strengthen the baby's lungs; a phone call was placed to let his dad know to get to the hospital. I was due to have another shot for his lungs twelve hours

MEKHI'S STORY

later. Twelve hours later never came. Well it did but I had already had him. The contractions came faster and stronger, but I was still able to pass time by sleeping. I woke up to the dullest, driest pain in the world. It was like pulling a molar tooth with no anesthesia.

All I could think was hold on one more day baby. Just one more day! You can do it. Hell! You had been counted out from the very beginning but nonetheless you fought. Stay one more day so that you could have a fighting chance. I knew doctors would count you if I delivered at twenty-three weeks and five days. Let us just make it to twenty-four weeks gestational age.

Mommy is sorry for all the pain she put you through. This baby had to fight for survival since entering my womb. Now I am on my delivery bed begging him to stay put for one more day. At one a.m. on September 24, 2015, I talked to myself, I apologized for all the times I let his father hit me and I apologized for not having the strength to leave him after he infected me in this pregnancy too. I apologized for putting my child last so that I may put a man first. Who in the hell do I think I am? I apologized for knowing what I was dealing with and still choosing to endure it. As my aunt would always say, "Well Tricky, you knew he was a snake when you picked him up". I am not a snake charmer but I damn sure tried. I remember feeling my baby trying to exit my womb so I arched my hips and squeezed my legs so tight, air could not pass.

Do you think for one moment that all my pleading, compromising and efforts to keep him in the womb did any good? No, it did not. At one

MEKHI'S STORY

twenty-two a.m. I got this feeling, like the beginning and the end all at once. I am telling everyone that it is time and the nurses are running around like chickens with their heads cut off trying to get suited for a delivery. It was quite a scene I must say. The nurses are yelling for me not to push. I have never been one to go against gravity. Some things you just have no control over. At this point, I only had to open my legs and let him slide out. He was coming whether we were ready or not. It was a very dry slide, but he came out at one twenty-eight a.m. I named him Mekhi (who is like the Lord) Amir (Prince).

This is for you Peanut!

MEKHI'S STORY

<u>Missing You</u>

In loving memory of an Angel that got his wings way too soon. You are truly missed my love. Not a day goes by that I do not regret the foolish decisions I made that ultimately claimed your life. I am forever remorseful for the role I played. Continue to visit me in my dreams my little fly in the window. Momma knows that was you!

Forgive me Mekhi

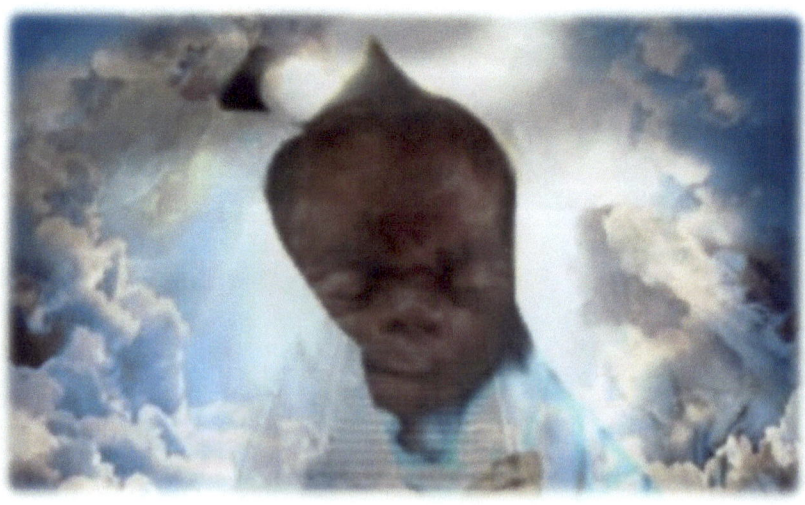

MEKHI'S STORY

September 24, 2015

CHAPTER 1

MOURN BIRTH

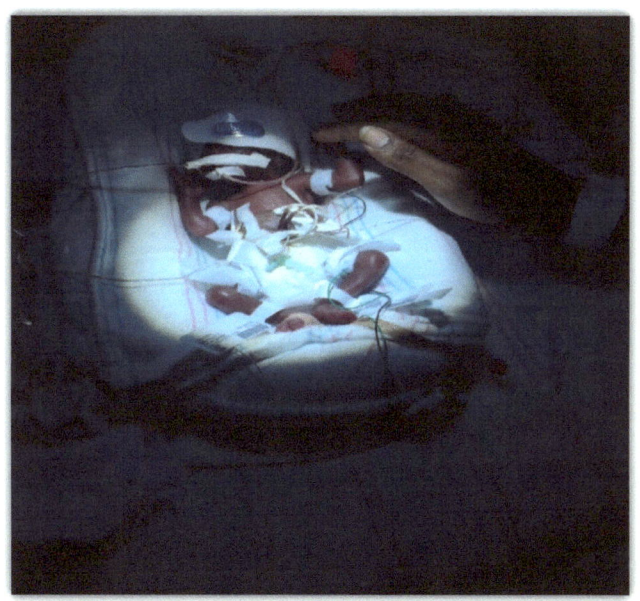

Facebook post: 6:17p.m. "Well Mekhi Amir Edwards made his debut this morning at 1:28a.m. One pound and four ounces. Total shocker but

MEKHI'S STORY

it is what it is. Pray for my baby, I'm at home pacing the floors until we meet again tomorrow".

Holy smokes little guy! You were the easiest delivery ever. You were born with a little peanut head. No, wonder why mommy always called you Peanut when I was carrying you. My other children came out with near white skin. However, you had a medium brown skin complexion. You had a perfect little big nose. Only one of your eyes had opened. It was the most beautiful grayish bluish color I had ever seen. The other was still fused shut. Your hair was laid down like flowing silk. Ten perfect fingers and toes. You had your father's scrawny ankles and knees, but you were breathtaking. I managed to notice all these details of you within thirty seconds of the doctor holding you up so that I could see you. You had been whisked away to be put on a ventilator to help support your lungs, or so I thought.

Nearly nine hours had gone by before I could see you again. Only God knows what they did to you in that time. I will never understand why my visitors got priority to see the child I birthed. I instantly felt cast out of your life by the hands of the nurses and doctors.

What had I done so wrong? Why can't I see my son? For hours, I sat on the hospital bed playing the blame game. All I could think about was the quality of life my child would have being born seventeen weeks early. Then I got my chance to see the child I gave birth to. I went into the nursery thinking I would hold you and never let you go. That was not the case. The tiniest baby that I had ever laid eyes on laid quietly in an incubator with patches over the eyes to protect them against the U.V. lights used for babies with jaundice. Cords and tubing ran all over my baby. Never in my wildest dreams did I ever think that I could give birth to a baby so small. He was one pound and four ounces. His Apgar score was a measly 2. At this point I am extremely terrified. To add insult to injury the doctors had the audacity to tell me that my son had a fifteen percent chance of survival for the first twenty-four hours. FIFTEEN PERCENT? What the hell do you mean sir?

That's my son in that incubator. What are you saying to me? He'll more than likely be dead by tomorrow? I didn't give birth for him to leave me so soon. Surely, you'll do something, right? He's been fighting all this time; just help him out a little. That's my boy Doc K. He is supposed to live. Before I left for the day all the doctors and nurses had given me their word that he would be ok. They said things like Mom, get ready; this is going to be a long four months in the NICU. I didn't care if it would be nine months. Just make sure my boy lives. Please don't count him out because he is the smallest baby in the nursery. Don't count him out because he was born to a poor aboriginal woman on Medicaid. Considering how far this world has advanced over the past 400 years, you'd think that saving a child's life would be important regardless to skin color and social class status. That is not the case. Well at least not our case.

If I am not mistaken his lungs had already collapsed once. Leaving him at the hospital murdered my soul but I was a single mother to six other children, and we had been living in a shelter. I had rules to follow. I

MEKHI'S STORY

vaginally delivered my son at one twenty-eight that morning and by five thirty in the evening, I was at home with the other children. Of course, I didn't want to leave my child with strangers, but the hospital didn't have a room to put me. All the rooms were filled. I never did buy that excuse. It seemed to me that I had picked the wrong day to show up to the hospital in black skin and on Medicaid. There really was no point in me being a patient. I paced the floor all night. What ifs and the how do I ran through my head the entire night. What am I up against? I don't know much about prayer, but I have some devout Jesus fans on my Face book page. Maybe they can lead me in prayer. I called on all my prayer warriors that night. I didn't know it then, but you can't ask everyone to say a prayer for you. Some people pray on your failures and demise. This would turn out to be a battle between me and the Lord. There would be a series of messages over the next few weeks that were only for me to get. No family member, no Facebook friend, no church chaplain or saint could prepare me for the series of unfortunate events that was to take place.

MEKHI'S STORY

September 25, 2015

CHAPTER 2

<u>We are Indigenous</u>

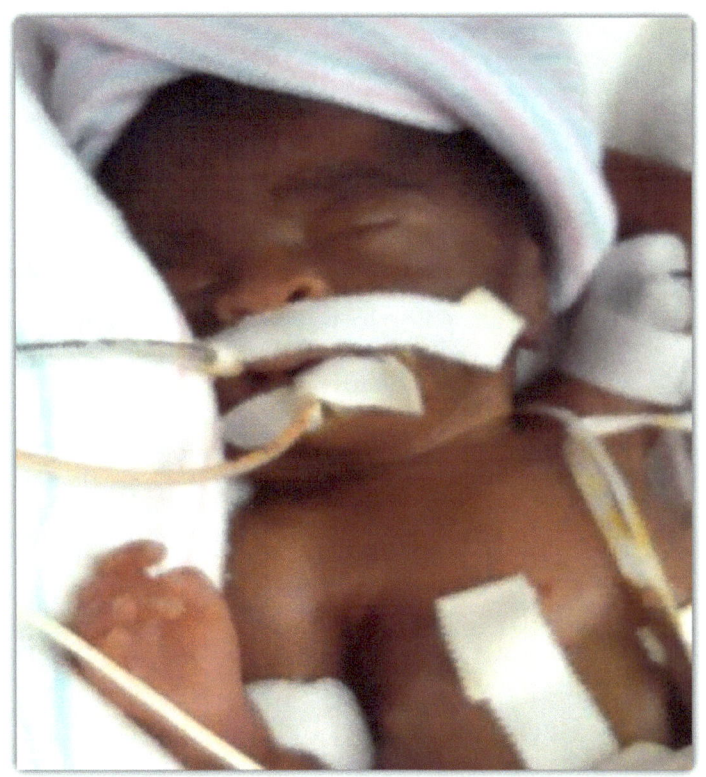

-

Facebook post: 9:22a.m. "Mekhi must know that he has a purpose. He is giving me so much hope. Twenty-four hours down and no more complications. Thanks everyone for their prayers.

MEKHI'S STORY

Facebook post: 11:22a.m. "MEET MEKHI (WHO IS LIKE GOD)"

"You thought I was worth saving

So, you came and changed my life

You thought I was worth keeping

So, you cleaned me up inside

You thought I was to die for

So, you sacrificed your life

So, I could be free, so I could be whole, so I could tell everyone I know

Hallelujah

Glory to God who changed my life

Forever

Because I a free, because I am whole

And I will tell everyone I know"

~Anthony Brown and Group Therapy

MEKHI'S STORY

As odd as it may seem, people have always said that when prayers go up, blessings come down. Maybe they are right. After walking into the NICU to see Mekhi, I approached his incubator and pulled the blankets back to see my little guy; laid back, just as cool as a cucumber, with his feet crossed. It was as if he was at a beach, trying to tan. Only he was in his incubator receiving phototherapy for jaundice. I smiled and told him that I'd be right back because I needed to have a word with the doctor.

"Hey Dr. K, a moment of your time if you will please". "Yes Ms. Edwards"? "Well, I was just wondering if there was any way that Mekhi could be pushed by a window where he could be exposed to natural sunlight". The doctor asked me what I meant and like a proud peacock with my chest poked out, I replied, "What works for other races does not necessarily work for indigenous people. We are children of the sun, aboriginal if you will; therefore, we need natural sunlight to help heal us. I was told no! Maybe I was too boastful and/or proud to be indigenous for his liking. I boldly said, "Well how in the hell do you expect aboriginal babies to heal from jaundice under artificial lights that causes cancer. Are these babies artificial"? No reply! Let me take the time to explain that I do not identify as black or African American. That's degrading to me. I am indigenous/aboriginal. There is a difference. When you know who and what you are, no one can tell you who you should be or try to convince you of what you are or should be.

MEKHI'S STORY

  Instantly I got the feeling that I had birthed my son at the wrong hospital. Children's National Medical Center was right across the parking lot. Perhaps it would have been better for Mekhi if I had just gone there and gave birth on the floor of the emergency room. They would have rushed him to their NICU and tried to save his life. After all, it is the nation's top pediatric facility. No child is turned away because of financial status or race. Many of his needs were not being met, even at just twenty-four hours old. I got the feeling that my social class status and color of my skin would ultimately lead to Mekhi's demise. It broke my heart to learn that only some lives were worth saving. When you receive Medicaid and if the cost to keep you alive exceeds what Medicaid will pay then some facilities will automatically rule you out. They wait on you to die knowing they can help. The guilt of not being wealthy consumed me. I was a lower-class citizen, living in poverty. In their eyes, I was just another statistic, a poor single black mother on welfare and Medicaid with a bunch of kids and no fathers. What put the icing on the cake was the fact that my skin tone was of a darker shade.

  Facebook post: 1:24p.m. "Head Sonogram is NORMAL".

MEKHI'S STORY

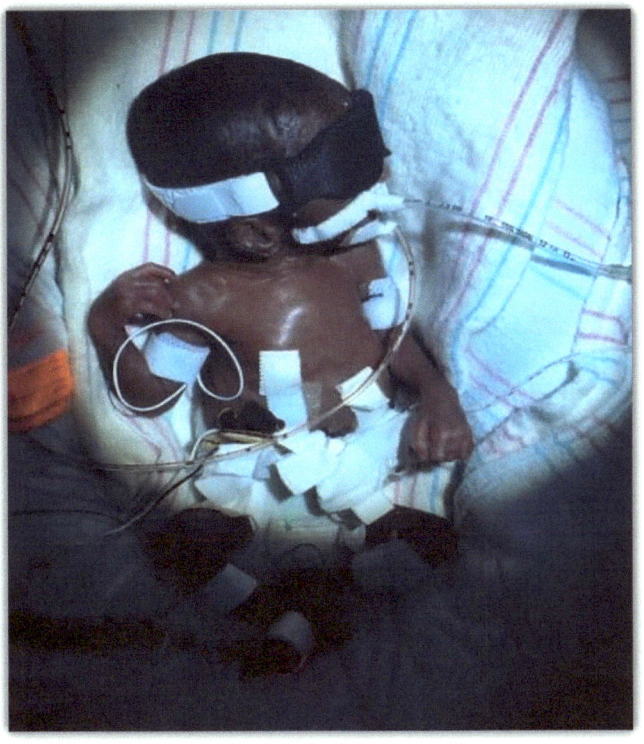

Heartbroken and lost for words, I returned to Mekhi's incubator and wept in silence. I know he felt my energy and perhaps that played a role in his quick deterioration. It's hard to fight back tears and remain strong while looking at an innocent infant giving it his all to fight for life. Hours had passed, dad and I were saying our goodnights. His father wanted to cheer me up, so he told Mekhi to raise his hand for mommy to let me know that he was okay. Surprisingly, Mekhi followed his father's command and raised the hand that was closest to me. My soul smiled and so did I. It was so obvious that Mekhi was alert and oriented times ten. My Peanut wants to live. I couldn't wait for tomorrow to come so I could visit him again. I can tell the story of a premature infant following commands at one day old until I'm blue in the face and no one would ever believe me. Lucky for me, I video recorded that moment. The video speaks for itself. Mekhi was gifted and one hell of a fighter.

It was a long and lonely drive back home. I was upset that I had to be at the shelter at a certain time. Here I am, a grown woman with a curfew. Mekhi is probably wondering why I had to leave. No child should be left alone, and I am hurt that the hospital did not extend courtesies to mothers of NICU patients. Over the course of the night, I had worried myself sick. I called the NICU every two hours for updates on Mekhi. Are they treating Mekhi humanely? Did they change his diaper? When will he have his first bowel movement? Are the nurses interacting with him? When will I be able to nurse him? He has been on an NPO (nothing by mouth) status since birth. I'm sure he's hungry. I used to eat like a pig while carrying him. He's starving by now for sure.

I pumped my breasts and labeled the milk before freezing it. After showering and getting the children's school clothes out for the next morning, I watched a couple of videos that I had recorded earlier in the day. Mekhi's dad and I was talking and playing with his hands. There's this one video where it looks like Mekhi was suckling on the tubing that ran through his mouth. There's a video of Mekhi stretching. Absolutely heartwarming, the way he put his hands up. It looked like he didn't want to hear anymore. I suppose he was tired. I called the NICU one last time for the night and was told that he was resting comfortably. Reassured, I went to sleep and after

MEKHI'S STORY

three hours I woke up to pain in my lower back. This was a familiar pain. It felt like contractions. As odd as it may sound, after the birth of my third child, I started having contractions in my lower back. I dismissed that pain because I was no longer pregnant. Maybe it was the bed. That's it! It was a twin sized mattress and I am a big girl. I ignored my body and went back to sleep.

September 26, 2015

CHAPTER 3

Comfy Much?

Facebook post: 11:02a.m. "You have any idea how hard it is to make a black woman smile? Weight of the world on my shoulders hidden behind a simple smile! Two days post-delivery! Feeling great! About to go see my Ki man!"

Two days post-delivery and I am feeling blah! It was the first time I had smiled since before giving birth. I literally feel like the weight of the world is on my shoulders. All I can do is mask that pain behind a smile. The truth is, I am afraid for Mekhi. I've never had a premature child, so I don't know what to expect. Nonetheless, my children and I are on the way to the hospital to see Mekhi. It must've been around noon when we arrived. As I mentioned before, the visitor's policy was strict. Only two of us could go back at a time. My eldest son Joseph and I went back first. When Joseph got sight of Mekhi, I could see the confusion, disbelief and concern in his eyes. He had never seen a baby so small. Nervous and scared, Joe delicately held Mekhi's left foot between his thumb and index finger. It was instant love at first sight. One thing is for sure, Joseph always protects his brothers; I knew that in that moment, a bond that could never be broken, was being formed.

After a few more minutes, it was time to rotate. Joseph left out so that Jayden could come in and bond with Mekhi. That went on until everyone got their turn to see their brother. I'll never forget the way Mekhi laid in his incubator with his eye patches on. He spread his fingers on both hands whenever any of us touched his leg or arm. That was an indication of just how alert and responsive he was. Who does this little boy think he is? Look at how he's lying in his incubator; so cool, calm and comfortable looking. Despite having ventilator tubes taped to his face, he looked at peace. It was the way his feet were crossed Indian style that made me laugh. No matter how many times I separated his feet; he still crossed them back, each time, moving as if I was irritating him. Mekhi looks like he is relaxing under the shadiest tree ever.

MEKHI'S STORY

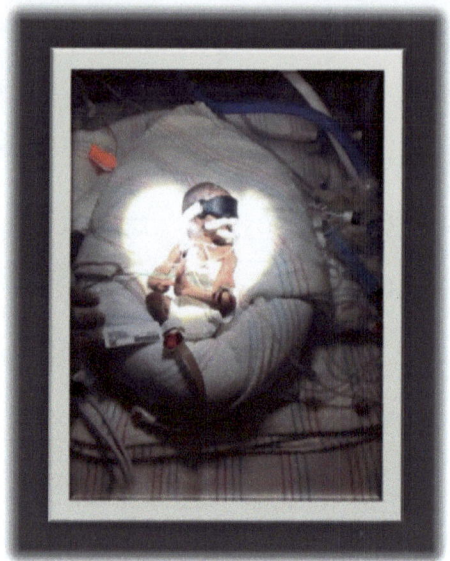

He had on the protective eye patches that looked like baby sunglasses and his hand slightly covered a part of his face. It was adorable to say the least. I hadn't seen his eyes since the day he was born, and I desperately wondered what he looked like and if his other eye had opened yet. I was about to find out soon.

At 12:54 p.m., the nurses took the patches off Mekhi's eyes and my heart melted instantly. My chocolate drop was full of life. His eyes were still trying to adjust to the bright lights, so he squinted and frowned a lot.

At 1:13 p.m., I recorded a video of him, and I said, "Hi man, wait until daddy see you. Wait until your daddy see you", as he waved hi to me.

Aunty Jennifer came to the hospital at 2:00p.m., and she was amazed at the amount of pint-sized personality he had.

At 3:09p.m., she took a picture of Mekhi and shared it to Facebook with a caption that said, "The new nephew… Him so little and already a fighter".

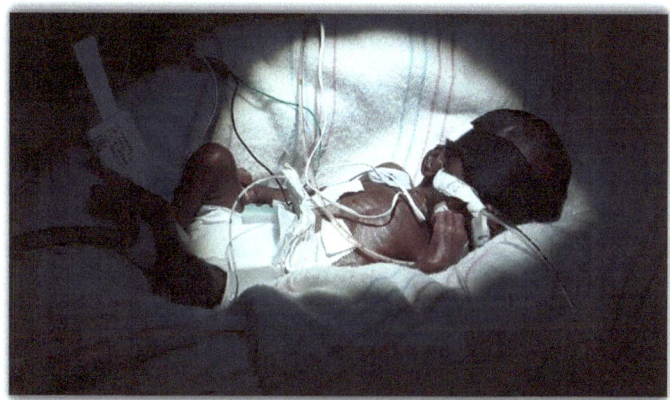

Many of her friends expressed that they would pray for Mekhi. Some people were concerned about the long road he had ahead of him. It was a long day for Mekhi and me. I just wanted to hold him instead of touching his feet and hands.

September 27, 2015

CHAPTER 4

<u>R. Kelly to D.C.</u>

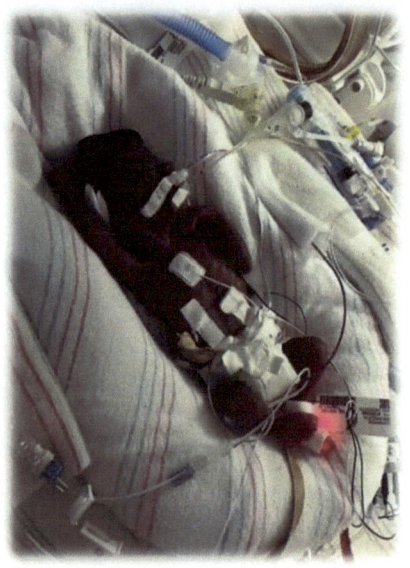

Facebook post: 3:47p.m. "Jaundice levels went down, ventilator settings went down, he is responding to light. He responds when you talk to him and touch him. Y'all did say when prayers go up, blessings come down! Well this non- believer is officially a believer".

A big part of me will always believe that fathers are little girls first loves. They have the potential to set the bar at what girls look for in men when they become of age. A father's love and presence are powerful. I wasn't so lucky to have that. My father spent majority of my life in and out of prison. Mostly in! When he was out, he wrestled with drug, alcohol and sex addictions. I have no solid recollection of growing up with my father past the age of five. Even though I loved my father, he was a walking nightmare. He abused drugs and women. It didn't matter that I was around and watched him. People like that, get their thrills off an audience, even if it's an innocent child. I am in no way blaming him for the way I turned out; I am simply saying that his presence in my life would have made a huge difference. He wasn't always bad. There are good memories. It's hard to raise a child while you're behind bars, struggling with your own addictions. It's hard to raise your child when you have your freedom and are dealing with drug addictions. Sometimes I understand his absence.

The streets are mean and easily influenceable. For nearly eighteen years of my life, I looked for a father figure in every man I chose to date. He had to be twice my age and had to be abusive. I grew up watching my dad beat my mother and every woman after her. The same abuse occurred for every man my mother was with after my dad. It was at an early age that I concluded that a man wasn't a good man unless he beat, cursed and abandoned you. This is what I saw often as a child and I was at a moldable age. They always came back with flowers or a gift, meant to serve as a peacemaker. One thing they always did was blame mom for their actions. The cycle continued with me. The innocent child grew up to be the abused victim.

MEKHI'S STORY

Facebook post: 6:30p.m. "I would like to thank Mr. R Kelly himself for the concert in DC last night. I haven't seen my dad since 2008. He met a few of his grandkids today".

My dad's time in DC was brief and I didn't want him to leave but I had much more important matters to attend to. My Peanut needed me, and I needed him. I was still trying to adjust to being a single mother, living in a family shelter while having a premature infant in the NICU. Life was hard and unbeknownst to me; it would soon take a tragic turn.

September 28, 2015

CHAPTER 5

15% Chance of Survival

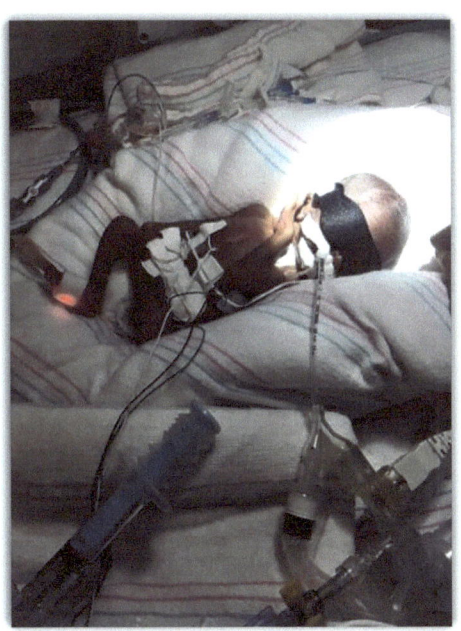

Facebook post: 5:03p.m. "Him looking so good. Doctors gave him a 15% chance of survival for the first 12 hours. He is four days old now. Won't he do it".

I am ecstatic. He is defying all odds. The doctors had all negative things to say about him being premature. Everything they've been saying

MEKHI'S STORY

has been going in one ear and out the other. They counted Mekhi out since birth and he is still here, fighting the good fight. Every test they performed on him, he passed. Peanut wanted to live. One thing that constantly concerned me was that he still hadn't had his first bowel movement. I have work experience in the health care field. I know that is a red flag. Every baby I've given birth to passed meconium for the first day or two. The doctors explained that since he was premature, his body was trying to play catch up. He was on an NPO or nothing by mouth status, so all I could do was pump my breasts and store it in anticipation of him having it once he could eat. In the meantime, he received artificial nutrients intravenously. I thought that was stupid considering I was a human cow, ready to feed him at any moment.

After a blood transfusion Mekhi had received, he looked like a brighter and more vibrant baby. When will I be able to hold him? I'm tired of sitting on this hard ass chair for hours, only being able to touch his hand or foot. Mekhi needs to know that he is not alone. Mommy is here and she loves you. The fact that he still hadn't passed stool worried me restless. Instead of going to the nurses with my concerns, I went straight to the doctors. "Hey, Mekhi is four days old and he hasn't had his first bowel movement. He also hasn't had his first milk feeding". The doctors had the audacity to say it was normal in premature babies. I worked in nursing homes and rehabilitation centers, so therefore I knew if it didn't come out the rear end then it would eventually come out of his mouth. The thought of him going through that, scared me. Nothing was making sense to me and I wanted my son to be immediately transferred to the Nation's Top Pediatric Facility just 20 feet from where he was.

September 29, 2015

CHAPTER 6

<u>I'm Okay Mommy</u>

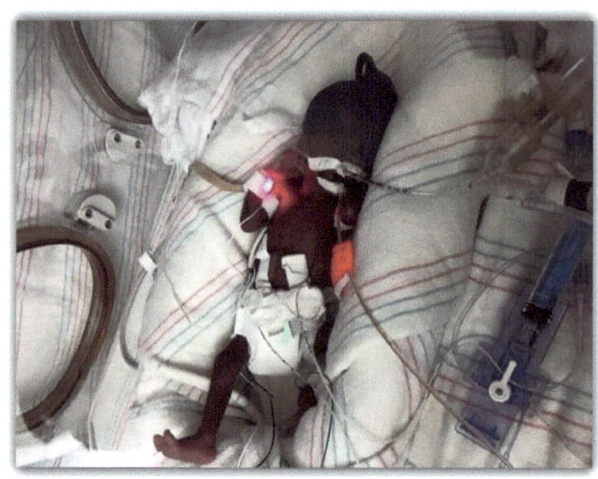

Facebook post: 10:33a.m. "This is going to be a long four months. I just want to hold him. He's opening his eyes and he tried to jump up while I was talking to him."

I pulled out my phone to record him and as soon as I started recording; he put his hand up, signaling that he was okay. My heart melted instantly and all I could say was, "Hi baby." Mekhi stretched his entire body and at 10:34a.m., I said, "Jeez, you have some big ass feet." A trait he inherited from me indeed. I was in awe at how alert he was. He understood everything. Mekhi reacted whenever the door to the NICU opened and closed. He turned his head to whatever direction he heard his name being called from. For years, I used to say, "something told me that something wasn't right, or I had a gut feeling that this was wrong." I know now that that was intuition. My intuition told me that Mekhi needed to be transferred to CNMC.

At around 11:00a.m., I walked out of the nursery and seen one of the doctors assigned to Mekhi. As we stood in the hallway outside the NICU, I asked if he had a minute to address my concerns. He agreed. "You see Dr. I'm concerned that Mekhi's needs aren't being met. I'd like him to be transferred to the facility next door as I believe they are better equipped to meet his needs. Some of my children haven't met their brother because of the age policy in the hospital. It's very hard and uncomfortable, having to stand at Mekhi's bedside. Keep in mind that I gave birth naturally just four days ago. My body aches tremendously and standing up six to twelve hours a day sabotaged my body and slowed down the healing process."

The doctor told me no. He said that, "When babies are that critical, CNMC transfers the baby to WHC. One reason being that WHC is smaller and more equipped to give the baby one on one care. CNMC is bigger and the nurses and doctors are assigned to several patients and Mekhi would not get personalized care." I had all types of questions as we stood in the

MEKHI'S STORY

hallway in front of a camera posted high up on a wall. The doctor dismissed me and turned to walk away. In that moment, my only thought was that my son would die there. How could they deny the transfer of an extremely critical infant? He deserves a fair chance at life regardless of his race and my social class status.

MEKHI'S STORY

September 30, 2015

CHAPTER 7

<u>*Fighting Temptation*</u>

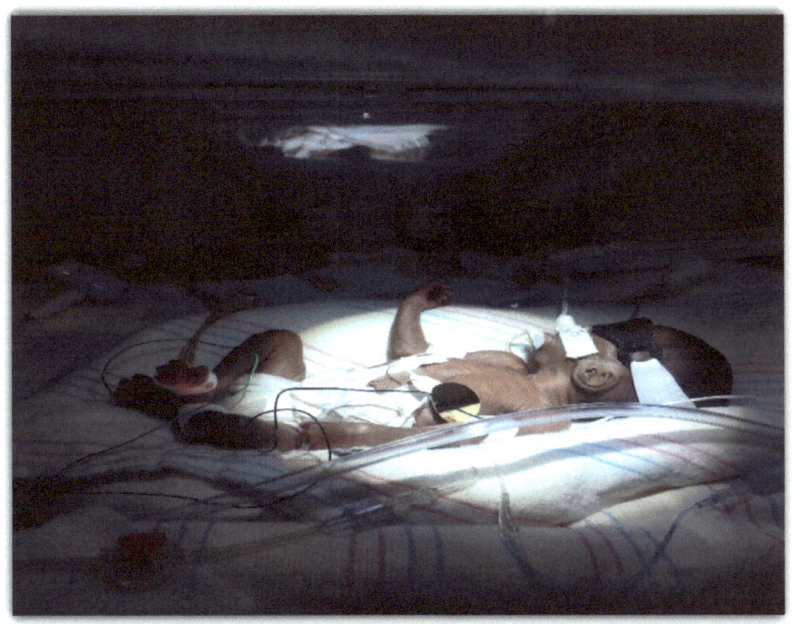

Dear Mekhi,

Even though you are laid in your incubator, appearing to look comfortable and content, my spirit tells me that you are experiencing discomfort. You are wearing eyepatches and I desperately want to see your

MEKHI'S STORY

face. I want you to know that I am here. You are not alone! My heart breaks just knowing I cannot hold you. You deserve to feel the love that is within me. As I sit by your bed, teary eyed, I wonder what's on your mind. Everything in me wants to remove your eyepatches and take you out that incubator to breast feed you. You need me. I need you! You deserve to feel the love that I have for you. You are not an experiment. These doctors and nurses don't mean you well baby. How anyone, that considers themselves to be human, could ignore a precious and innocent baby boy's needs is beyond me. There are no words that can express the outrage and pain I feel. Why won't this hospital transfer you to the facility next door. Something is going on in this place. Maybe I am the wrong shade to be taken seriously. It's 2015, color still be an issue! You're an innocent baby boy. You'd have to be an animal, sent straight from the pits of hell to deny an infant his right to quality medical care. To make matters worse, you still haven't pooped. This is the first time in the history of me living, that I have heard or seen of an infant living past 5 days without having a bowel movement. Looking at the care that every other baby in the nursery is receiving, I can honestly say that it is not the doctors and nurses to save your life. Regardless of how I am feeling, I'm going to do my best to remain positive. I'm team Mekhi, even if no one else is baby boy. Your mommy loves you and recognizes the fighter in you.

With all Love and Hope

Your Mommy

October 1, 2019

CHAPTER 8

"MI FAMILIA"

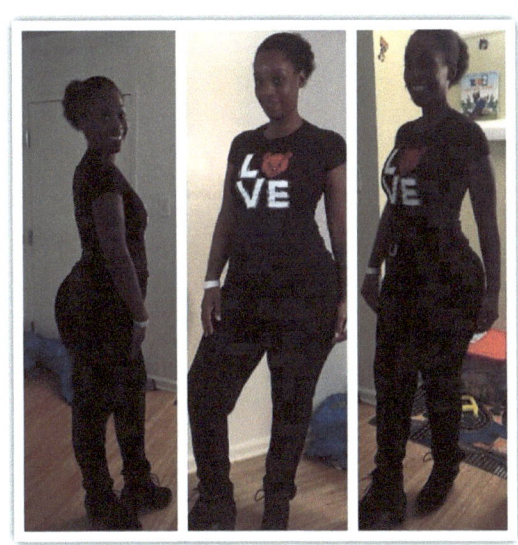

Facebook post: 10:44a.m. – Exactly one week since I gave birth. This rain is about to be torture on my hair.

This morning's rain was depressing. Nonetheless, I remain as positive as I can. I forced myself to take a shower. Barely washing the parts of me that mattered most. I just wanted to see my baby and learn about all the

MEKHI'S STORY

progress he made overnight. Afterall, today's a new day, right? I forced my hair into a ponytail and went outside to get in my truck; stopping to take a picture. Nervousness takes over my body as my other children came outside to pile into the vehicle. Immediately upon arriving at the hospital, everyone falls into routine. The youngest twin and I go back to wash our hands and visit Mekhi. That went on until I was down to the oldest child.

At 12:25p.m., I snapped a picture of my baby. He was laid under those jaundice lights, with his eye patches on. Mekhi looked to be comfortable. My mind and spirit are at ease.

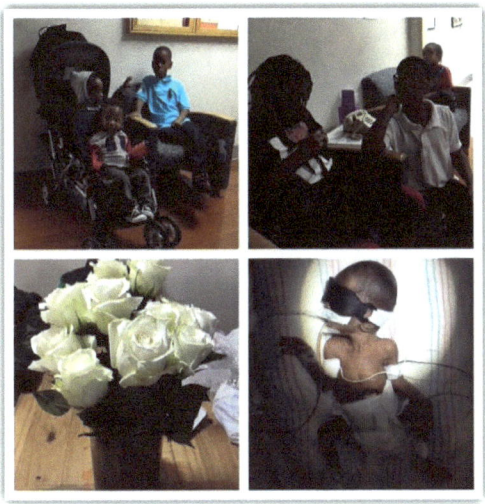

Facebook Post: 2:07p.m. – And if GOD got us, we gon be Alright. Mi Familia

Today was the second time in my life that I received flowers. The first time was a few months ago, a dozen of pink roses, just because it was a Tuesday. I happened to meet someone while I was pregnant with Mekhi. Today he got me a dozen of white roses. How pure is that? There's nothing but good news to be heard about my sonshine. I decided to take your brothers and aunt out for lunch.

Facebook Post: 3:40p.m. - @ Golden Corral Buffet and Grill. Field Trip

MEKHI'S STORY

    I couldn't eat much baby boy. I keep feeling contractions in my lower back. Even though I just left you, I miss you. I still haven't held you. You still haven't had a bowel movement. What am I to think at this point? Before going home, I called the hospital to get an update. I was told that he was resting, and I had nothing to worry about.

October 2, 2019

CHAPTER 9

Lost for Words

Facebook Post: 3:09p.m.- The life just left my body. Mekhi has an active brain hemorrhage on both sides of his brain. "JESUS BE A ROCK".

Something happened to my baby overnight. A thief came in and stole my baby's comfort and joy. How can a healthy baby boy go from okay to critical overnight? What happened to my sonshine? My Peanut? Who in the fuck mishandled my seed? The doctors are saying that it is normal for a premature baby to show all normal signs for the first week of life. Some shit about a "honeymoon phase". My sweet innocent boy has a grade 4 IVH on the right side of his brain and a grade 2 IVH on the left. He didn't have this the night before. What happened? I'm lost for words. One week of nothing but good news for the most part and now my world is being torn upside down. I called everyone I could think to call. We cried, we prayed, and we swore up and down that these doctors didn't know the God we served. I sat at my son's bedside, lost for words, hurt that I could not comfort him. I just want to hold him. A part of me still believes that my touch could heal him.

MEKHI'S STORY

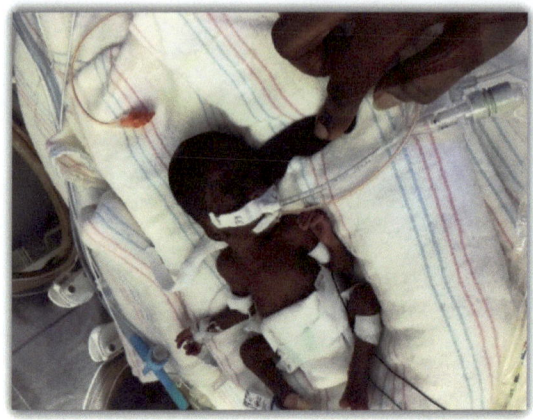

Your Aunt Kit came to visit you. To my surprise, she recorded a video of a nurse trying to clear your lungs, (even though they were already clear). The nurse went down too far and punctured something. You jumped in shock or pain. This concerned me enough to come back to the hospital. My mom called her pastor to come and say a prayer and offer a healing touch.

Facebook Post: 9:20p.m. – Pastor L. Paige from Zion Church came through and read scriptures from the bible and prayed over Mekhi. I want to thank my sisters, Jennifer Jlo Landis and Kyerrial Gordon for being there for me during my time of need. I also want to thank someone very dear to me, Mr. Robert Williams, for his continuous prayers and constant reminders to bring patience with my faith. I love you all. RIGHT NOW, LORD.

MEKHI'S STORY

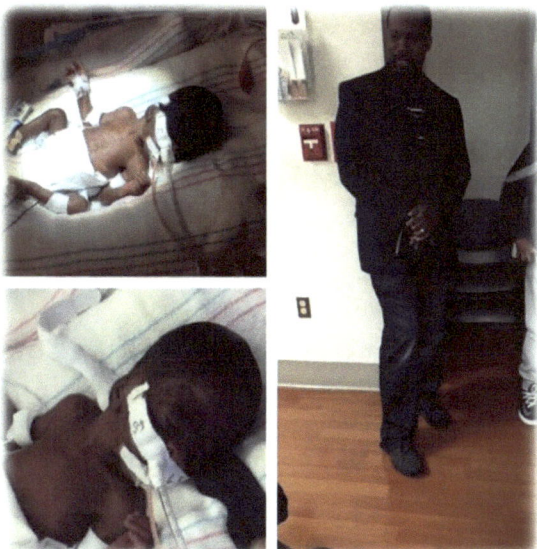

October 3, 2019

CHAPTER 10

IS THIS N.E.C.?

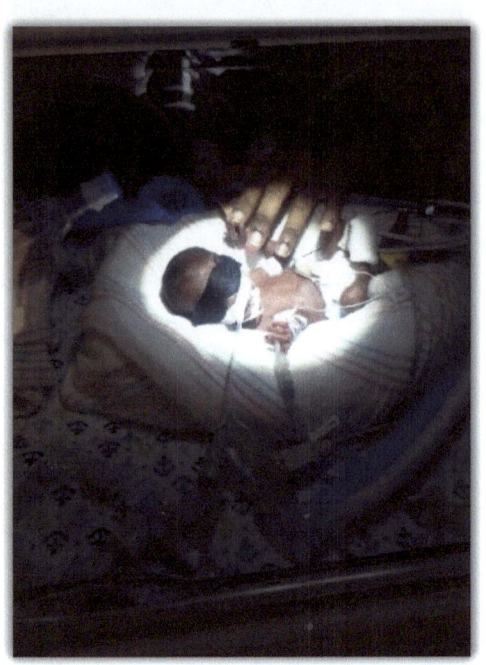

"You look different. It's only been hours since I last saw you. A sausage like patty popped up in your abdomen overnight. Since I can't hold you, I pulled my phone out and googled, sausage like patty in premature infants' abdomen. Necrotizing Enterocolitis was the first thing that came up. My soul left my body as I read the details of this disease. Of course, I brought it to the attention of the doctors and nurses. They dismissed it off as gas even though all your X-rays showed no free-flowing gas moving.

MEKHI'S STORY

Facebook Post: 12:02p.m. – Where you at God? I want to believe that you didn't send Mekhi in this world to suffer (but he has been doing just that). Questions ran through my head like, why give him to me if your plan is to take him away? What kind of God am I serving? Is this fair? Is this just? Why don't you reveal yourself? Show up and show out like everyone claims you will. What's the meaning of this? My baby's lungs collapsed in the wee hours of the morning, he had to be resuscitated. It took five hours to stabilize him. You never realize how precious life is until it is lost. Thank you to my brother Jonah and sister Danisha for coming to be with Mekhi and I at four this morning. Love has no limits. I was and still am a complete mess, scared to leave, scared to sleep, thinking I will miss a call from the doctors. This is absolute torture! All I keep thinking is, will I ever get to hold him (not lifeless)? Will his brothers get a chance to meet him? Should I prepare myself for the worst? How tf do you do that? Are we fighting a losing battle? Should I let him go if this should happen again? If he survives, what quality of life will he have?

MEKHI'S STORY

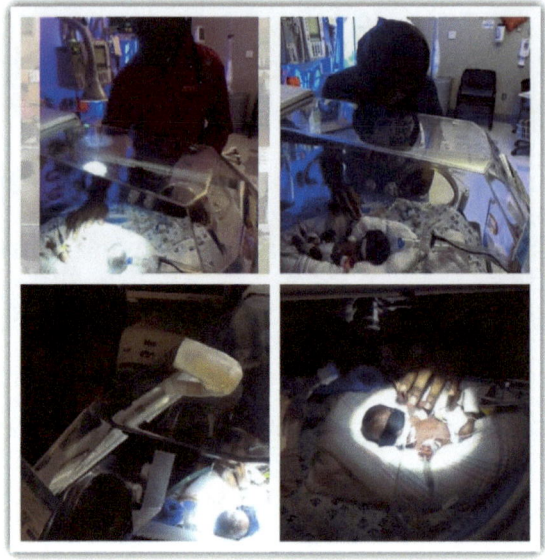

Facebook Post: 5:53p.m. – For over 20 years, I felt unloved and unwanted by this man. I always felt like I had to compete for his love. This morning at 5, he called to check on Mekhi, and I couldn't even talk because the tears and emotions consumed me. He said, "Oh no, I'm on my way baby girl!" Stubborn me was like, "you full of it". Sure enough, at 3pm, he called to say he was at the hospital. All the hate, resentment and anger quickly subsided, knowing that he was here for his only child in her time of need. He came with his lady friend from Chatham, Virginia just to comfort me and see Mekhi. I've never felt prouder to finally call this man my father! Of course, my sister, Jennifer, nephew and kids were in step. Man, I love these guys to death. Being there to keep me stable means a lot to me.

MEKHI'S STORY

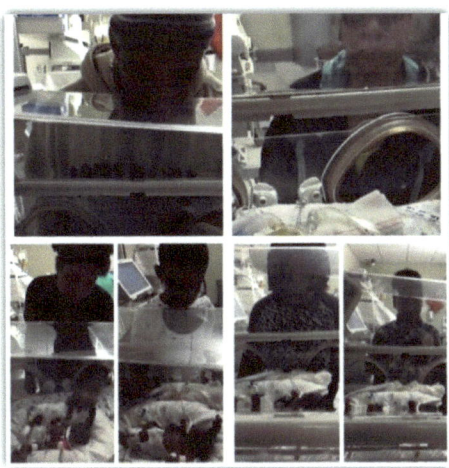

Facebook Post: 9:00p.m.- My baby with his eye open looking like him daddy.

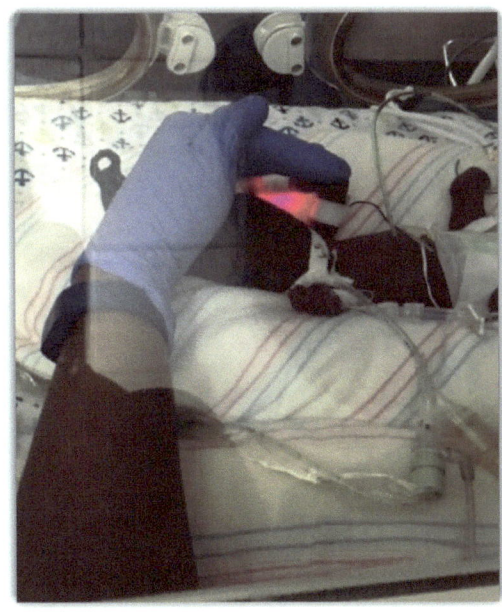

MEKHI'S STORY

I spent a total of 13 hours at the hospital, desperate for things to turn around for the better. Only God knows what's in store for my baby.

October 4, 2015

CHAPTER 11

Labor Pains

There was something about last night's sleep that was unsettling. I tossed and turned all night. Pain in my lower back kept me from sleeping. This pain is familiar. It reminds me of all my pregnancies. For some weird reason, I've always had contractions in my lower back, instead of my abdomen. I wonder if it's because I have a retroverted uterus. To sum it up, my uterus is backwards. I relate this feeling to something being wrong with Peanut.

Facebook Post: 5:44a.m.- I've been having labor pains since 4a.m.! This can't be good. I'm no dummy, something is wrong.

A friend commented and said, "Go to the hospital". I replied, "I'm here. It was the baby with complications.

Facebook Video Post: 8:14a.m. – Momma is not a fool, even though I'm not carrying you, I can still feel when something is wrong baby. The acid levels in his body are up, which is a sign that his organs are shutting down. God... WHERE YOU AT? You said all I need is a mustard seed of faith. The selfish part of me wants him to keep fighting, but the mother in me sees that after 10 days of fighting, he is tired. Mentally preparing myself to let him go, let him rest in perfect peace.

MEKHI'S STORY

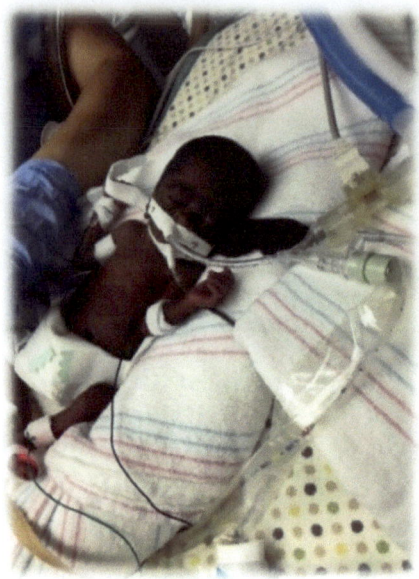

I don't think my heart can break any further. Watching a baby fight for his life, while the doctors and nurses do everything they can to aid in his deterioration, made me so angry. I can't begin to wrap my mind around why these "medical professionals" won't transfer my baby to the pediatric facility right next door.

"Its 8:14a.m. and time to take your protective eye patches off. I recorded a video of that moment and to my surprise, I see that your eye is swollen, and I'm saddened to hear the excuse behind it.

MEKHI'S STORY

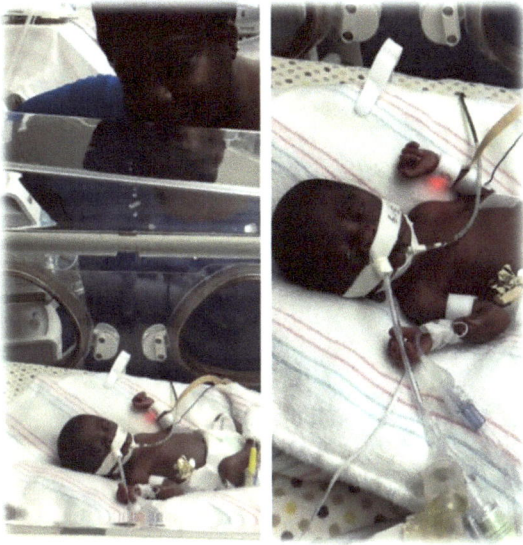

Facebook Post: 1:14p.m. – My dad and stepmom came early this morning to sit with us a few hours before they got back on the road. They left at 10:30a.m. and about an hour and a half went by, he called to check on us, but Mekhi's lungs had collapsed again. He was worked on and stabilized. I was talking to my aunt because she had just come in and sang to my baby. I happened to look up and seen my father standing over me. They turned around to come and support me once more. I've given birth six times; all vaginal, four of them natural and this is by far the worst pain I have ever felt. Its all smiles when you are preparing to bring life into the world. You don't really prepare for death until you are face with the possibility of it and even when you are, you still don't know! I'm fighting for you Mekhi. We will give each other something to fight for.

MEKHI'S STORY

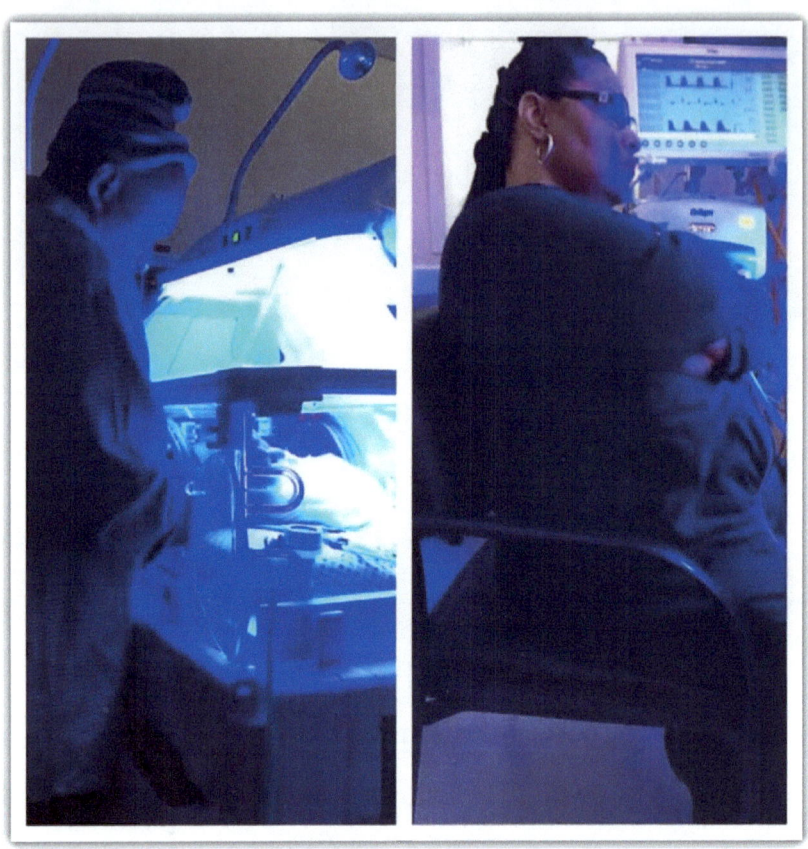

October 5, 2015

CHAPTER 12

Color Matters

My son's tubing is displaced, and you can see it in his face that he is in excruciating pain. It's weird. Whenever there is a weekly update for him, the doctors never tell where they messed up. They insist on placing the blame on the parents. His PICC line was in the internal jugular vein and it needs to be repositioned. Do you think there is a sense of urgency to help my son? There wasn't. You see! Every day, color and social class status shows me that there is a difference in the quality of care an individual receives. It's sickening, but this is the world we live in. It doesn't have to be this way. He's an innocent baby boy. I really feel that these people are afraid of the greatness in him. They are going to block his shine. I see it and feel it.

Facebook Post: 11:17a.m. – This warrior is defying all odds! It's been said that weapons would form but THEY WON'T PROSPER! Glory to GOD. Jaundice is gone, blood tests looking normal. He is responding very well to the antibiotics for pneumonia. He's having a chest and abdomen x-ray right now. Praying for some more good news. How many prayers can this fighter get? This guy got more fight in him than most people I know, including me. God and Mekhi are preparing me for something. Time will reveal.

MEKHI'S STORY

#turnitaroundlord #prayforMekhi

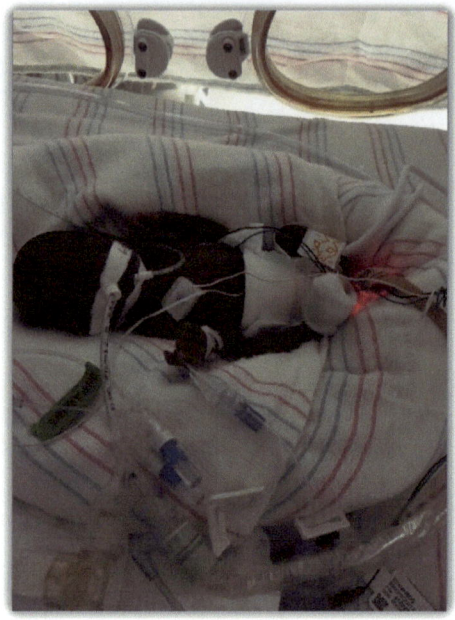

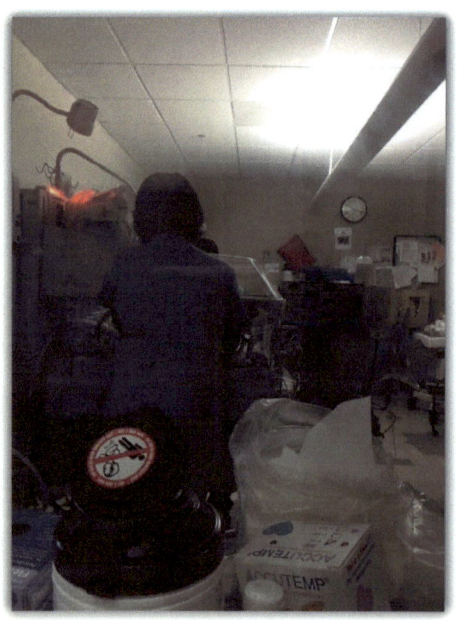

MEKHI'S STORY

Facebook Post: 9:51p.m. – Trust in God. GN FBF! Continue praying for Mekhi. This single parent thing is hard, but I got you. Thank God your aunt and Grandma are so supportive so I can get to you.

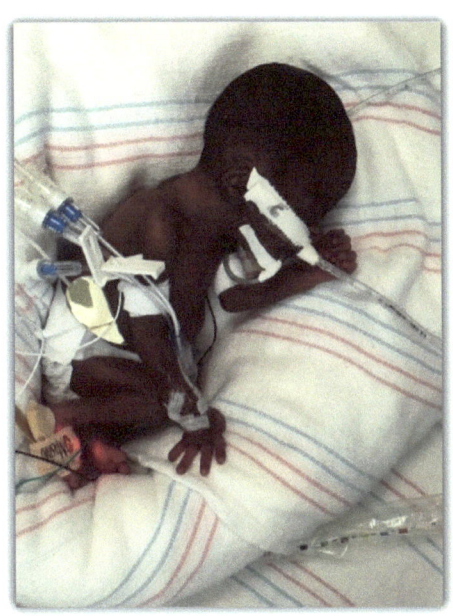

Let me explain; for the most part, everyone that is brought into this world has 2 parents. In this phase in my life, Mekhi's father checked out. I guess people handle grief differently. Rightfully so, maybe he blames himself for our son's early arrival. He wasn't there as much as he could've and should've been. Life has a way of proving that the things we make the most time for, is the shit that doesn't matter. Life is short and were all going to learn that soon enough. You can't put your arms around a memory, so I want to be by his side as much as possible. Mekhi's paternal aunt and

MEKHI'S STORY

grandmother had agreed to watch 3 of my other children so that I could visit my baby. I am eternally grateful. Sitting here with my child for 10-12 hours a day are well worth it, and I wouldn't trade it for the world. I only wish that I could hold my son so that he could feel the love that's in me to give to him. He hasn't been attached to me since 9/24/2015. I know he misses me and feels unloved.

October 6, 2015

CHAPTER 13

Excluded

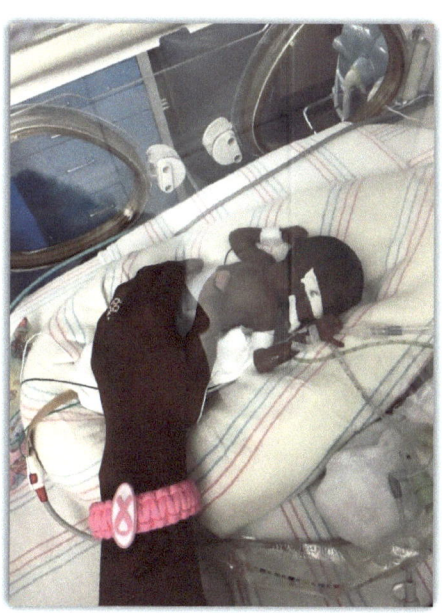

Facebook Post: 8:51a.m. – GM FBF. He is still fighting. Day 12!

Facebook Post: 9:37a.m. – Tuesdays are always the hardest for me. Family rounds with the doctor. The day parents ask all the questions and get all the updates straight from the Doctors mouth. I'm

MEKHI'S STORY

tired of being asked by the nurses if dad is coming. All these babies with loving mothers and fathers around them being held and cuddled. I'm sitting here, by myself as always, in tears looking at Mekhi through an incubator window. Just wondering when I can finally hold him, when will I hear his first cry, see him smile? No one can answer these questions because he is so critical. This is hard, its hell on earth. No more than I can bear. When will this nightmare end? I'm barely making it.

Facebook Post: 3:54p.m. – Fell asleep driving again today! Time to park the truck and ride Metro until I get it together. For my sake and others. Looking for a side view mirror.

I'm not sure what it is with me and car accidents, but I always crash when I get close to my destination. I was driving up Naylor Rd and I woke up to a loud crash. I ran into the side of someone's car causing my side view mirror to fall off. I am mentally and physically exhausted. There is no way I can be in two places at one time. I have stretched myself completely thin. Bathing and grooming myself became something that I had to remind myself to do. That's how bad it was.

October 7, 2015

CHAPTER 14

DRAINED!

I'm too tired to even move a muscle. After dropping the children off to school, I went to the hospital just to sit for a while. For some reason I get the feeling that my baby doesn't want to be bothered. It hurts but I understand. I took a few pictures of him and rubbed his body before leaving. Maybe he will be in a better mood later.

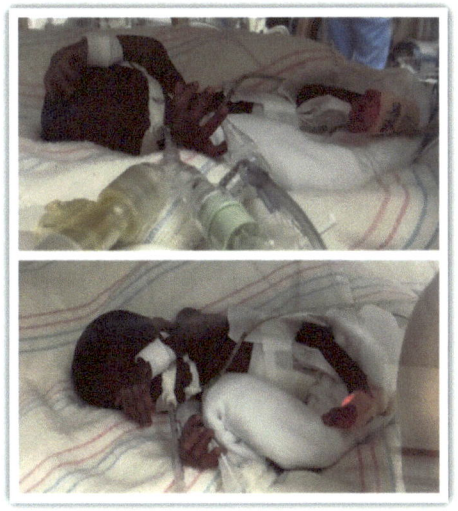

MEKHI'S STORY

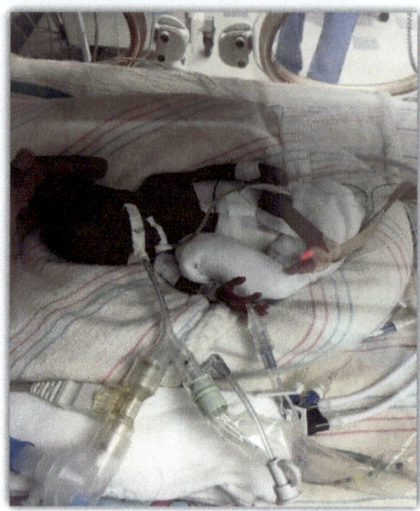

      I called the NICU to check on Mekhi. "Mom, he's resting, you should get some rest too". Those words comforted my soul and I went back into a deep slumber. I woke up just in time to get the boys from school. Thankfully I am recharged and want to spend time with my other children. It's not that I don't want to see Mekhi, I just hope that he would be alright one day without me. I helped the children with their homework and then cooked. I can't tell you when the last time I cooked was. Nightfall crept up on me and I decided to hit the hay. Not before checking on my sonshine once more.

      Facebook Post: 9:34p.m. – I had to share this update because I found it so funny. I called to check on Mekhi because I'm too tired to go see him and the nurse told me that he was fighting and kicking her. Whenever she does his cares, he would side eyed her. Just what I said earlier. He doesn't want to be bothered today.

The time is minutes to 12a.m. and I get the same lower back aches that told me something was wrong. I called the hospital and was informed that his lungs had collapsed but he was stabilized. Why didn't they alert me to this?

October 8, 2015

CHAPTER 15

ERUPTION

Facebook Post: 7:53a.m. - It was so hard smiling this morning. GM fbf!

MEKHI'S STORY

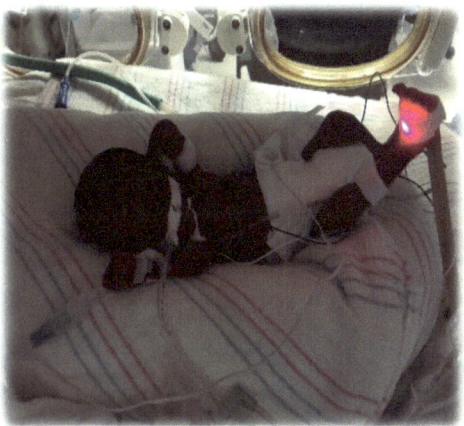 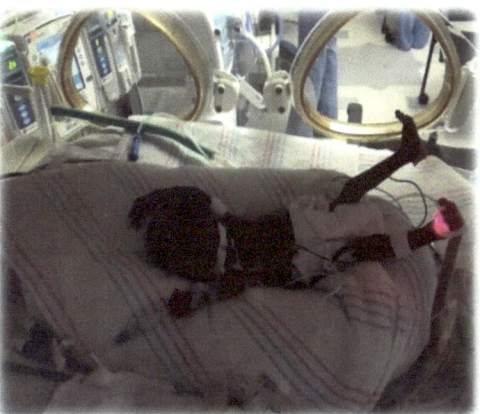

At 915a.m., I decided to record a video of my baby because the facial expressions he was making told me he was in pain. To my horror the one-minute video captures his intestines rupturing and the photos above shows his discomfort. He slid to the bottom of the incubator. It's absolutely unbelievable how they are doing my son.

Facebook Post: 12:25p.m. – Three days of good news and now I'm hearing nothing but bad news. I will hold onto your hand as we prepare for whatever it is to happen. GOD PLEASE TURN IT AROUND!

MEKHI'S STORY

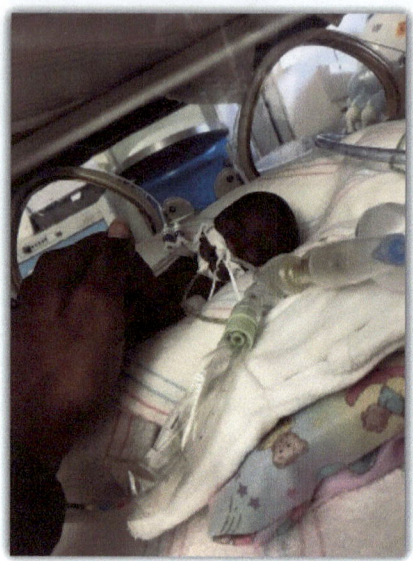

The brain hemorrhage didn't get any better. It increased a stage. My mind checked out as I studied the picture I had just taken of Mekhi. If you're as observant as I am, you will see a full trash container. It's always like this. Full linen and trash containers every time I come in. Sure, I asked for housekeeping to come and remove it so that I could sit on that side in comfort. Of course, I was ignored. In other news, my brother Jonah and his friend Bender came to pick up all the boys today and took them to play basketball and play videos. He turned his van into an arcade/movie theater, with fancy lights and all.

Facebook Post: 7:17p.m. – So happy that they enjoyed themselves with their uncle today.

MEKHI'S STORY

Family pulling together in time of need is what matters most. There is no way I can pull this off all on my own. I'm not afraid to ask for help when it's needed. Pride is a sin. This whole experience has offered me numerous lessons in pride and ego. It also showed me that I had been selfish as well. What right did I have making my son suffer? I knew he was suffering. I see the look in his eyes, and it is devastating to watch daily.

October 9, 2015

CHAPTER 16

HEAVY BURDEN

Today I was hit with some hard news. My son will not be getting any better. In fact, he's getting worse. I am at a loss for words. All I can do is stare at my son. Tears flowed, and my emotions are all over the place. These doctors and nurse most did something to my son. It's 4a.m. and I ask the nurse if I can hold him. The bitch had the nerve to say, "not right now mom, he's just too critical." At this point, all the anger raged out of me and I replied, "Well bitch, if he's going to die anyway, what fucking difference does it make"? I was put out the hospital that day. As I walk down the long corridor, thoughts flood my mind. Take the baby and run to the pediatric facility next door. Run until you make it. Don't look back and don't back down from anyone.

The only thing that's keeping me from doing that is the fact that Mekhi is on a ventilator. How far could I get without his lungs collapsing and him dying in my arms? I watched the hospital professionals kill him off daily. If I had attempted to save his life by removing him from that hospital then I would be deemed a killer, not them. All of this because I showed them the video from the day before of his intestines rupturing. They dismissed it off as gas. That was not gas. All these days later and Mekhi still hadn't

MEKHI'S STORY

passed his first bowel movement. I blame myself. I should have never come to this hospital. What was I thinking? My God, I can't stand to be away from him. I know he is so lonely and in a world of pain. If I didn't have other kids, I would kill myself. The things that these eyes have witnessed has changed me forever. My son deserves a fair chance in this world. The reality is these medical professionals pick and choose who to play God to. It's not fair but, this is America. Race has and will always matter.

MEKHI'S STORY

October 10, 2015

CHAPTER 17

No Pictures Mommy

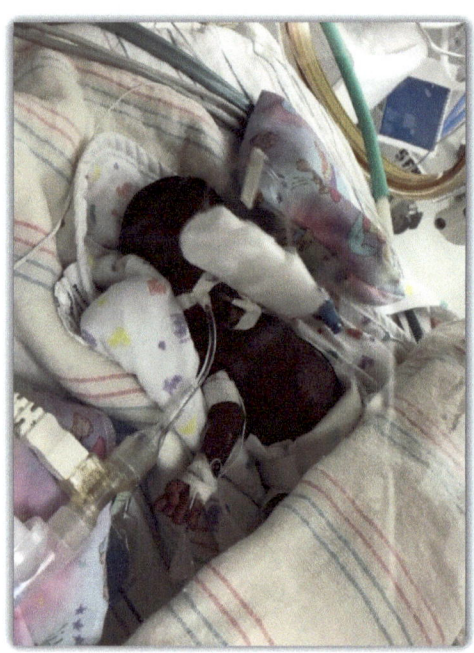

Look at my son man! Look at the pain he is in. Look how hard his abdomen is. This all started the night of October 2, 2015. Thank God I take pictures and record videos daily. He's deteriorating. Why did they have to do my son like this? God sees all and their day will come where they watch their love ones suffer in agony. This is unbelievable. It's so hard to sit here and watch him suffer in silence. I can no longer contain these emotions. I'm a strong woman but even rocks crumble. I cry out in silence while recording a video as my son watched me.

Facebook Post: Can you see the pain in his eyes? Whatever pain he is feeling is keeping him from resting! His next few hours are very critical, and this is a life or death matter. As a mother I don't know what to say or do. I don't want to be selfish and keep him in pain and I don't want to quit on him even though he is doing all the fighting. WHERE YOU AT GOD? GOD HEAR MY PLEA! SPARE MY BABY! Take away his pain! Do something. I can't take seeing him suffer.

MEKHI'S STORY

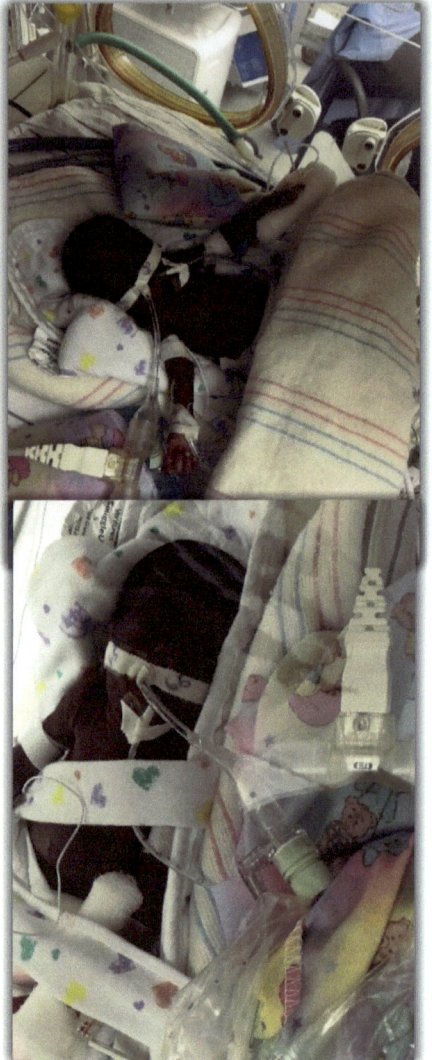

You see the pain in his eyes. Ask yourself this, what decent human being would deliberately torture a newborn infant to death? I am unable to be strong. All I can do is shed tears. There are no words that I can think of to comfort my baby. "Just end his pain, God"!

MEKHI'S STORY

October 11, 2015

CHAPTER 18

Joseph's Party

It's my oldest son's birthday today and I would like to be able to spend time with him even though Mekhi is terminally ill. My sister and I threw a last-minute party to celebrate his 13th birthday. As I hung decorations and taped balloons to the wall, my cell phone rang. It's the hospital. Hopefully they are calling to say that Mekhi improved over night. That's not the case. Mekhi's lungs collapsed and he flat lined. They wanted me to come right away because they knew he wouldn't survive. This is so unfair. I never got the chance to hold my son while he was alive. I was robbed! I got to the hospital sometime after 8a.m. and I did not leave until after 10p.m. Mekhi's dad and I finally got the chance to hold our son. I was in tears as I begged them to let me hold him. The pregnant doctor rudely says to me, "You know what, do you want to hold your baby?" That's all I've been asking for Dr. Could you please put us somewhere away from everyone? This is an extremely intimate moment. I do not want to be around all these healthy babies and holding my child knowing he would die. My request was not honored, and I was pushed near the full trash bin and dirty linen container. After some hours the trash was removed. I'll share those photos.

MEKHI'S STORY

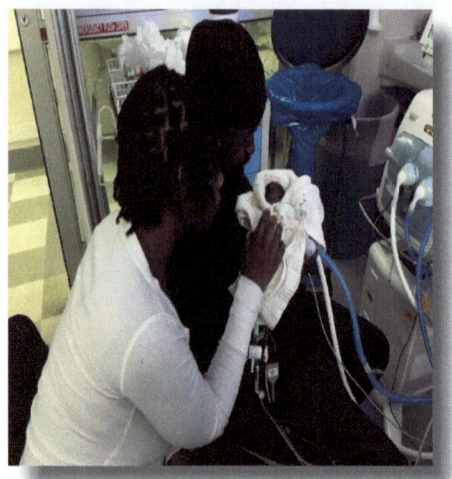
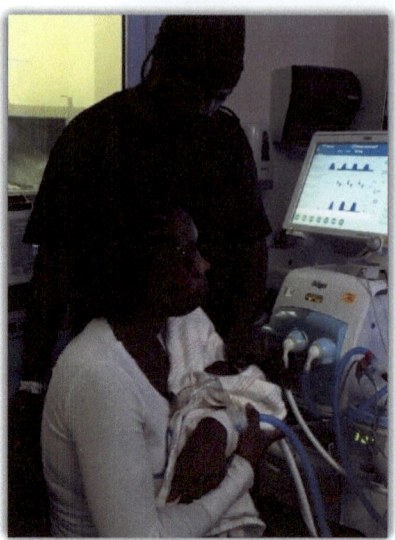

MEKHI'S STORY

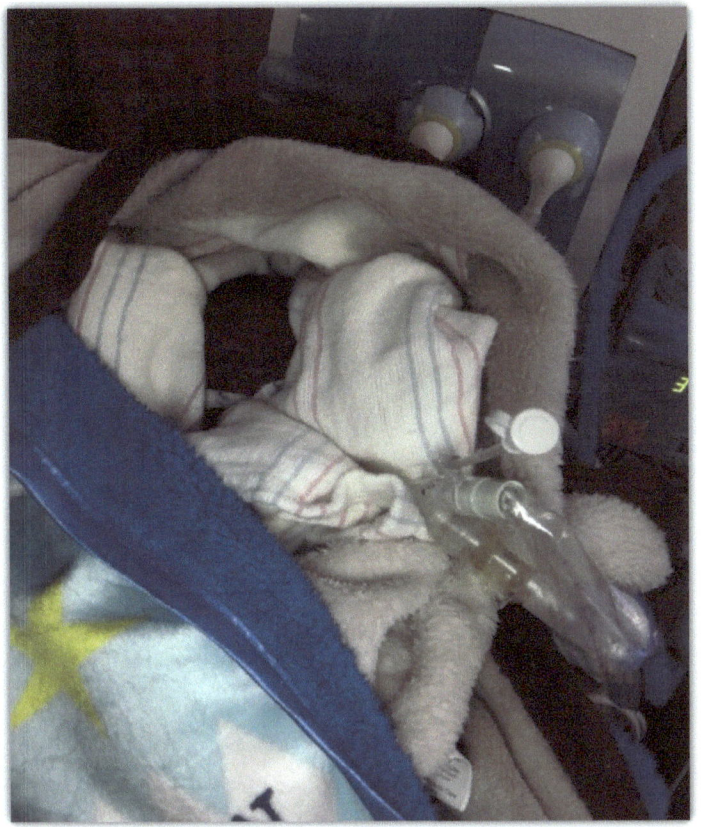

MEKHI'S STORY

October 12, 2015

CHAPTER 19

Free at Last

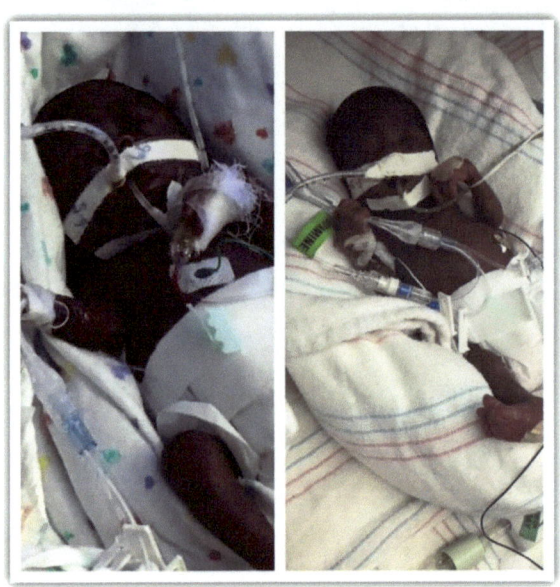

Facebook Post: 12:21p.m.- What a difference a day can make. The left photo was yesterday and as you can see his kidneys had shut down. As I was taping balloons on the wall for my oldest sons' birthday. The doctors called me and told me this was it! I went to the hospital and held

MEKHI'S STORY

my baby for three hours and we talked. The fear of losing my youngest son on my oldest son's birthday killed me. The photo on the right is today and he looks like a new baby. My faith was tested yesterday, and we prevailed. Thanks for all the support from everyone especially Jennifer Jlo Landis who had all the kids and helped throw my oldest son a birthday party. Thanks to Jauquinna Kelly and Jazmine Kelly for being there to help support the twins! Mekhi is finally about to be transferred to Children's hospital where God can continue performing miracles. RIGHT NOW, LORD!!

My love bug is being transferred today. My mind is racing all over the place. It's as if he's being freed from prison. I eagerly sign the discharge papers so they could hurry the transfer up. At 12:42p.m., the ambulance came to transfer my boy.

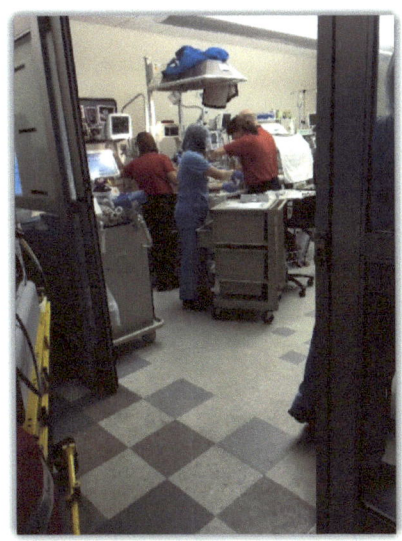

MEKHI'S STORY

At 1:30p.m. we arrived at the other hospital and they began working on him immediately. At 2:15p.m., Mekhi had a stomach X ray that confirmed my suspicions of Necrotizing Enterocolitis.

MEKHI'S STORY

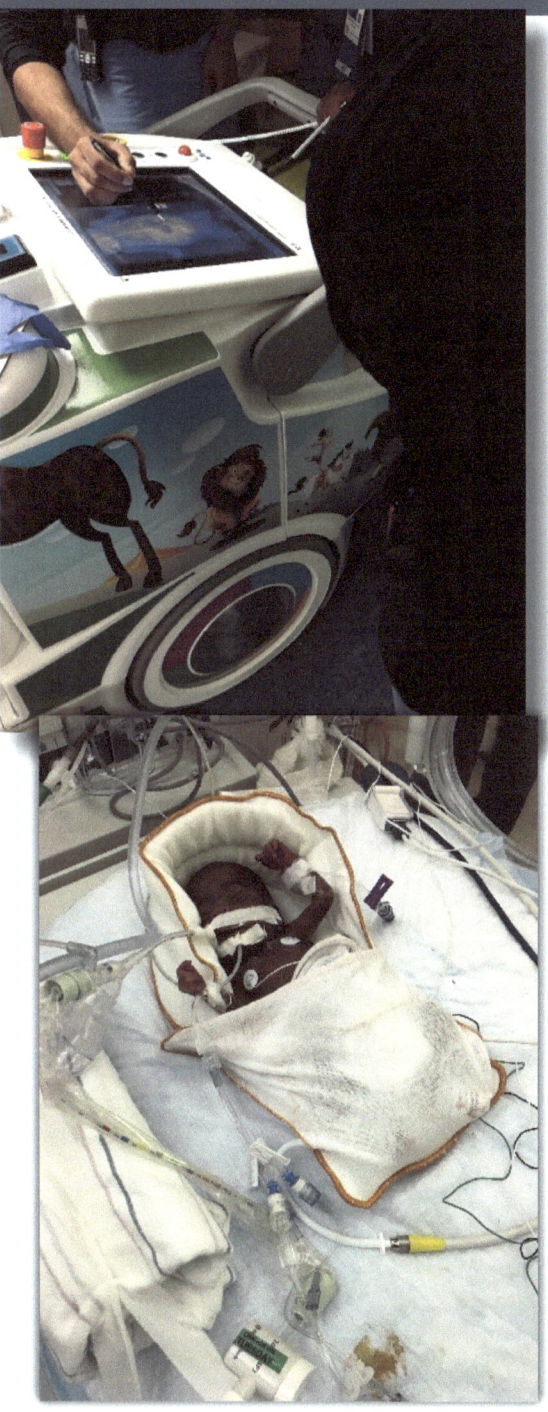

MEKHI'S STORY

Facebook Video Post: 7:55p.m. – Keep my baby in your prayers tonight as he prepares for his first surgery. God please guide the surgeon's hands.

The doctors think it's Necrotizing Enterocolitis. They want to be certain so they asked if they could do an exploratory surgery to confirm their diagnosis. Not even 15 minutes went by before they called me back upstairs with devasting news. It most certainly is Necrotizing Enterocolitis. It has advanced and all his intestines are dead, and the disease spread to his other organs. My mind went blank. This could have been avoided. The surgeon said, "I'm sorry but there is nothing we can do. I wished he had gotten to us sooner." WTF!! So that's it? I shared the news with family, and some came to be with me. The hospital chaplain came to pray over him, and you could see the fear in her eyes when she looked at my son. He didn't look human anymore.

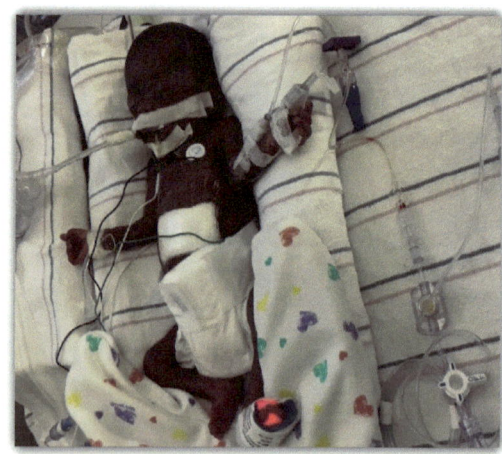

MEKHI'S STORY

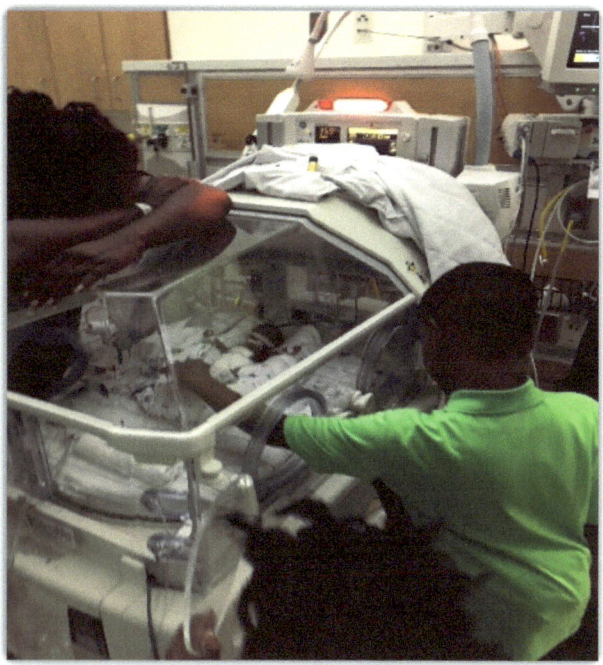

All we can do is pretend to be strong while our hearts break. Look at Mekhi's dad. That news hit him hard. None of us experienced anything remotely close to this.

October 13, 2019

CHAPTER 20

Lost for Words

Even though were at a different facility, the care and treatment are still the same. The lead doctor keeps rushing me to pull my son off the incubator since there is nothing, they can do for him. I still get the vibes that color matters. I see the same neglect and truth be told I am disgusted. I walked in to see my son out of his pamper and a dirty diaper near his feet.

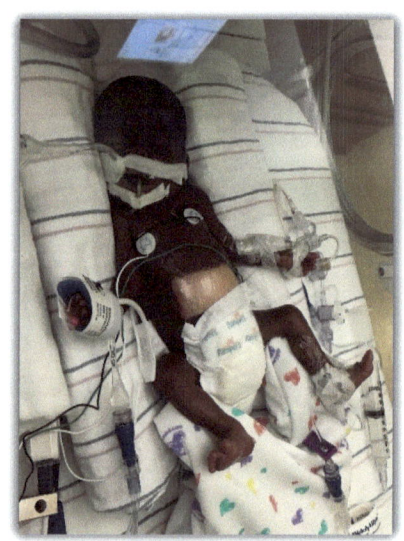

MEKHI'S STORY

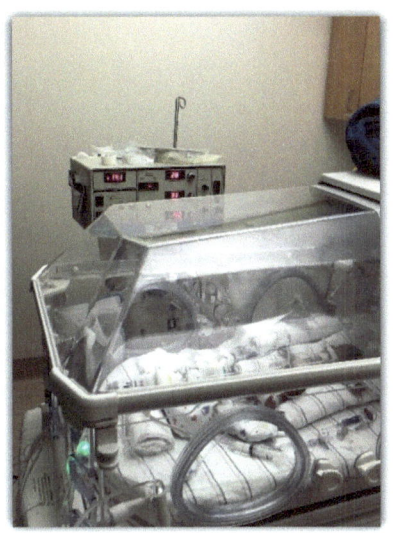

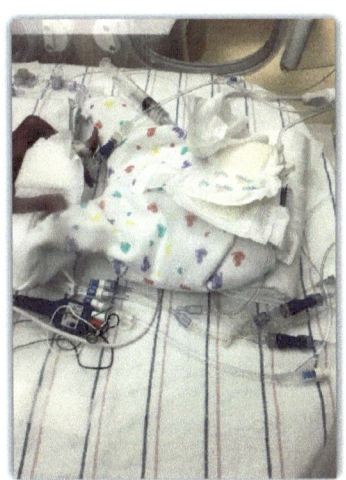

MEKHI'S STORY

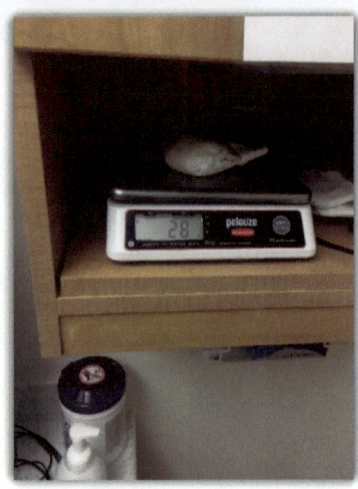

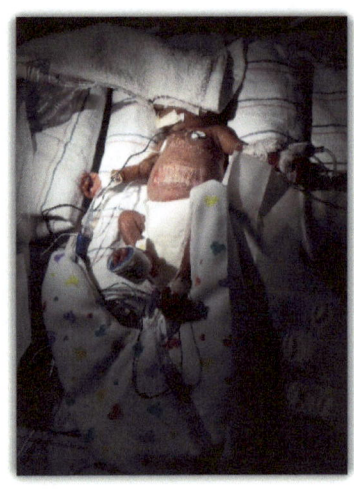

MEKHI'S STORY

October 14, 2019

CHAPTER 21

One Wish

Today is my 31st birthday. There's nothing in this world I want more than to hold my child and I got that wish. I held my baby on and off for about 8 hours, only returning him to his incubator to bring his body temperature back up. The doctors are still urging me to pull the plug, but I won't do it. A part of me is waiting for a miracle to breeze by.

Facebook Post from Jennifer: 7:29a.m. - 2DAY IS MY SISTER'S BIRTHDAY AND SHE CAN'T ENJOY IT LIKE SHE SHOULD OR DESERVE. UNFORTUNATELY, SHE HAS TO SPEND HER DAY WORRIED ABOUT MEKHI BUT GOD DEFINITELY DOES THINGS FOR A REASON. I AM TRULY HAPPY THAT THIS YEAR WE WERE ABLE TO ELIMINATE THE ROOT OF OUR PROBLEM AND ARE NOW ABLE TO BE SISTER AND BE THERE FOR ONE ANOTHER. WITH THAT BEING SAID SCREAMING HAPPY BIRTHDAY TO Chiquita Nicole Edwards

MEKHI'S STORY

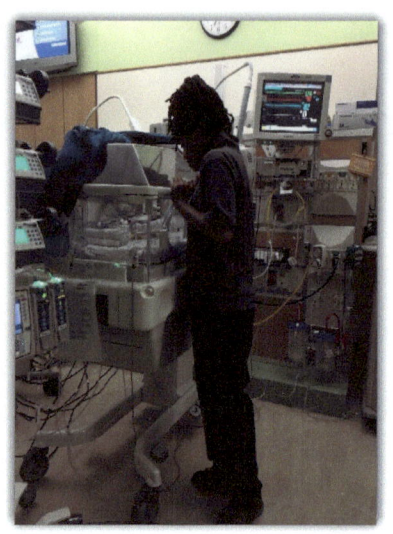
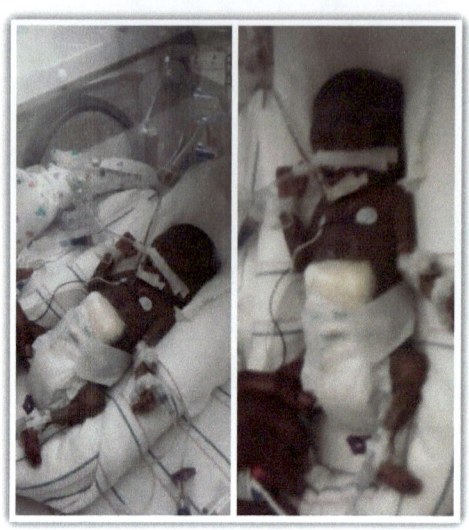
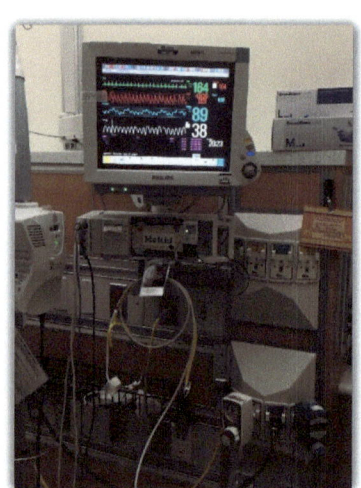

Facebook Post: 2:59p.m. - So, my spirit grows faint within me; my heart within me is dismayed. I spread out my hands to you; my soul thirsts for you like a parched land. Answer me quickly, O LORD; my spirit fails.

Do not hide your face from me or I will be like those who go down to the pit. Let the morning bring me word of your unfailing love, for I have put my trust in you. Show me the way I should go, for to you I lift up my soul. Psalm 143:4, 6-8

AND GOD SAID

I will lead the blind by ways they have not known, along unfamiliar paths I will guide them; I will turn the darkness into light before them and make the rough places smooth. These are the things I will do; I will not forsake them. Isaiah 42:16

~The Holy Bible~

MEKHI'S STORY

October 15, 2015

CHAPTER 22

Pray on It

Facebook Post: 12:51p.m. - The Valley of Dry Bones

37 The hand of the Lord was on me, and he brought me out by the Spirit of the Lord and set me in the middle of a valley; it was full of bones. 2 He led me back and forth among them, and I saw a great many bones on the floor of the valley, bones that were very dry. 3 He asked me, "Son of man, can these bones live?"

I said, "Sovereign Lord, you alone know."

4 Then he said to me, "Prophesy to these bones and say to them, 'Dry bones, hear the word of the Lord! 5 This is what the Sovereign Lord says to these bones: I will make breath[a] enter you, and you will come to life. 6 I will attach tendons to you and make flesh come upon you and cover you with skin; I will put breath in you, and you will come to life. Then you will know that I am the Lord.'"

MEKHI'S STORY

7 So I prophesied as I was commanded. And as I was prophesying, there was a noise, a rattling sound, and the bones came together, bone to bone. 8 I looked, and tendons and flesh appeared on them and skin covered them, but there was no breath in them.

9 Then he said to me, "Prophesy to the breath; prophesy, son of man, and say to it, 'This is what the Sovereign Lord says: Come, breath, from the four winds and breathe into these slain, that they may live.'" 10 So I prophesied as he commanded me, and breath entered them; they came to life and stood up on their feet—a vast army.

11 Then he said to me: "Son of man, these bones are the people of Israel. They say, 'Our bones are dried up and our hope is gone; we are cut off.' 12 Therefore prophesy and say to them: 'This is what the Sovereign Lord says: My people, I am going to open your graves and bring you up from them; I will bring you back to the land of Israel. 13 Then you, my people, will know that I am the Lord, when I open your graves and bring you up from them. 14 I will put my Spirit in you and you will live, and I will settle you in your own land. Then you will know that I the Lord have spoken, and I have done it, declares the Lord.'"

MEKHI'S STORY

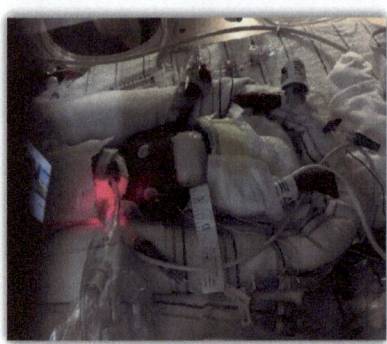
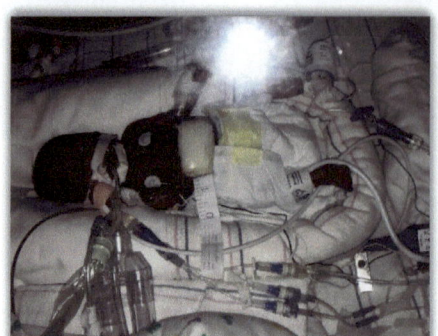

Facebook Post: 8:59 p.m. – Keep praying for Mekhi. This stuff hurts like hell. Doctors say that he is terminally ill. They don't know the God I serve though.

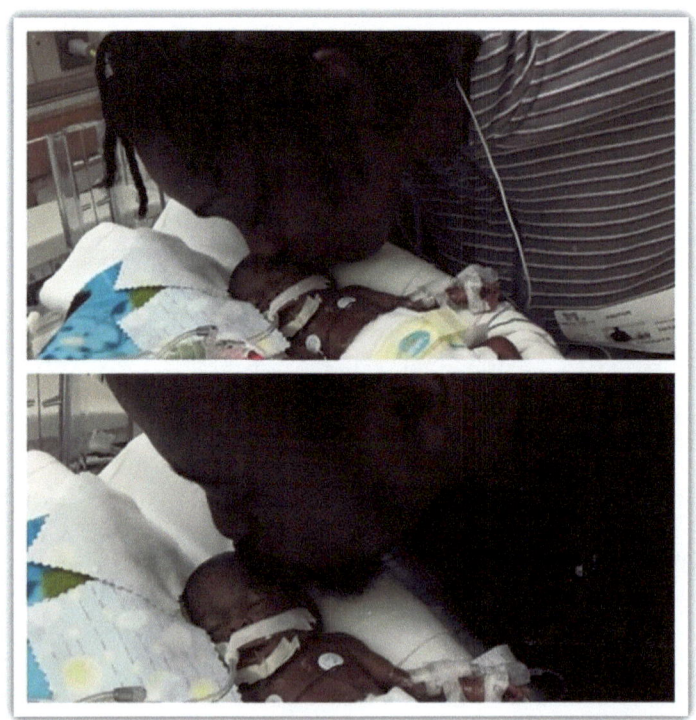

October 16, 2015

CHAPTER 23

Making up For Lost Time

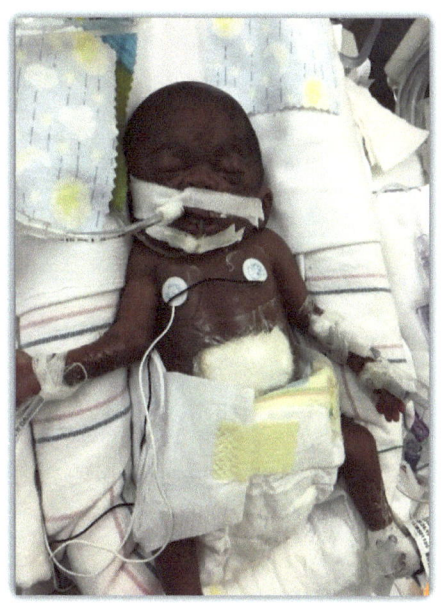

Facebook Post 10:59a.m.- "Cast not away therefore your confidence, which hath great recompence of reward. For ye have need of patience, that, after ye have done the will of God, ye might receive the promise."

Hebrews 10:35-36

MEKHI'S STORY

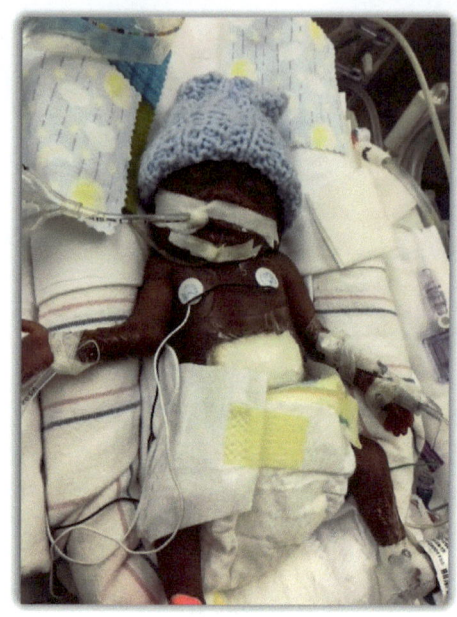

Doctors say this maybe it. Are we fighting a losing battle peanut? After watching his near lifeless, fluid filled body just lay there My heart told me to hold him. When I did, I watched life fill his body. Look at the white lines. My heart tells me to keep fighting with Mekhi. Should I lose him while I hold him, I will be ok with that because we got our time (however little it may have been). He knows he is loved. Pray for Mekhi!! "For Christ also hath once suffered for sins, the just for the unjust, that he might bring us to God, being put to death in the flesh, but quickened by the Spirit:"1 Peter 3:18 KJV

MEKHI'S STORY

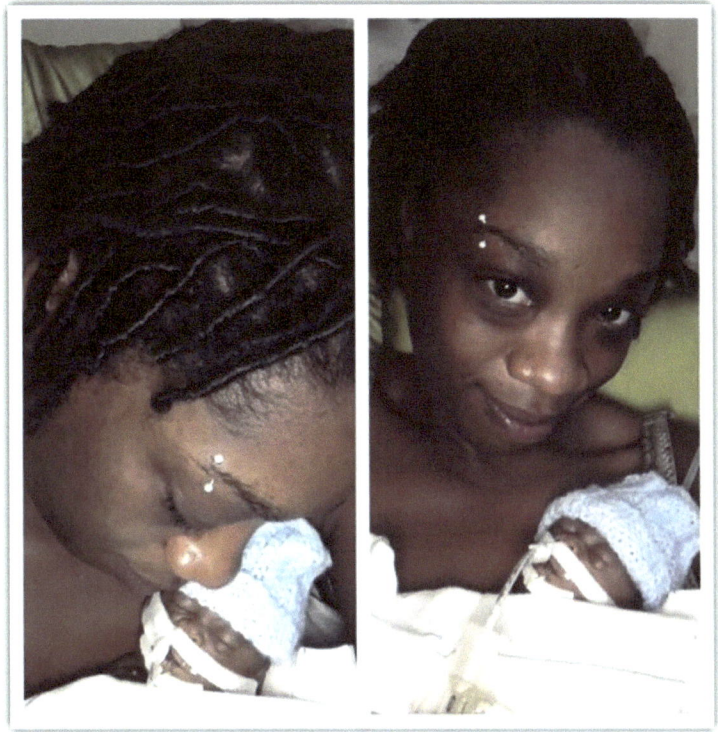

Facebook Post: 12:34p.m.- I never want to let go. I've missed so many days holding him since his birth. Tuning into Pastor Keith Battle as we move in unison in this rocking chair. How do you make up for lost time??

MEKHI'S STORY

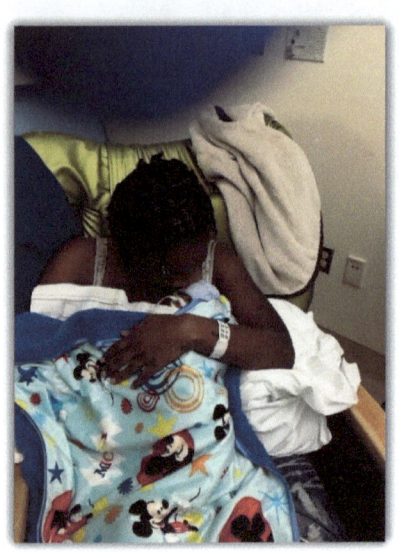 

Facebook Post: 5:27p.m- The hardest part about this whole ordeal is that I still have to find strength to carryon for them

October 17, 2015

CHAPTER 24

Still Fighting

Facebook Post: 5:07a.m. - The pain I feel in my heart is keeping me from sleeping. I sit up looking at pictures of Mekhi wishing things would have went different. This is a lesson of knowing when to let go and as you can see, I fail. No mother should be put in a situation where they give up on their child. That's the most painful feeling ever. Sure, I hear what the doctors are saying but its opposite of what I see my baby doing. Or am I fooling myself? If this isn't God's will then why hasn't he called Mekhi home? Don't leave me to make that decision because as you can see even with all odds against him, as a mother I chose life and I believe miracles can happen. But one thing this has taught me is that I need to clean up my life because I want to see my angel again. There is always a testimony in a test. I've been paying attention to the visitors since birth and I believe he was sent here to touch the lives of everyone who visited him. My eyes have seen so many revelations since his birth. Message received loud and clear God. Call him home now! I've been stubborn all my life and I really don't mean to rush your work or will BUT!!! RIGHT NOW, LORD! End his suffering.

MEKHI'S STORY

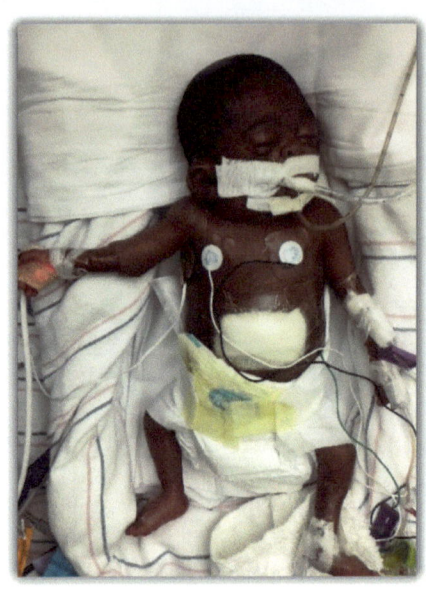

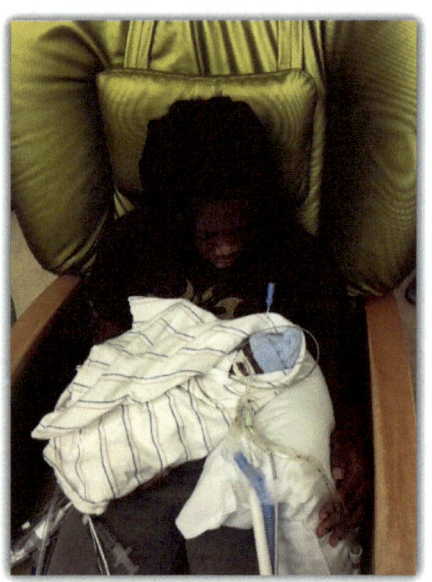

MEKHI'S STORY

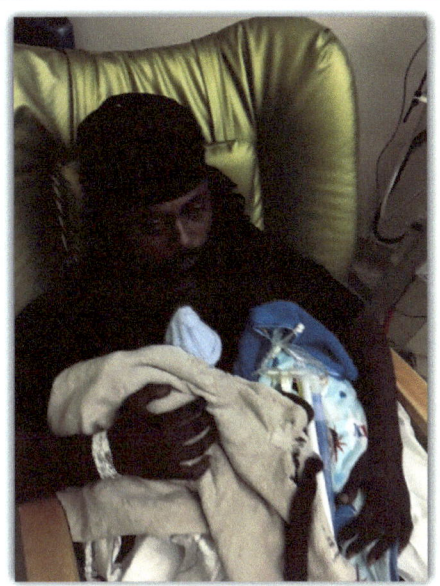

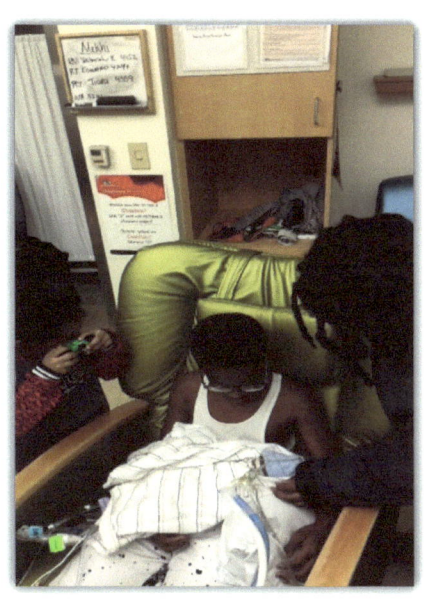

MEKHI'S STORY

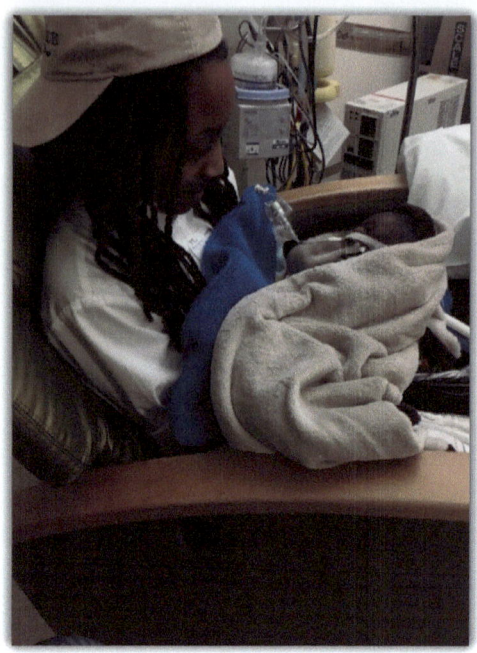

Even though the doctors said he would not live, I'm still seeing signs that he is trying to live. Who am I to cut his life short so the staff can use the ventilator for someone else? There is a reason why the staff and social worker keep coming into this room to ask me if I had made up my mind. I lost my shit! "Stop coming in here rushing me to pull the plug on my child. That's my son, I yelled." He had his first bowel movement today. Two as a matter of fact. The doctors said it was because of the vibrations from the ventilator. I don't believe that. He's been on the ventilator since birth. Why today?

October 18, 2015

CHAPTER 25

All Hope Lost

Facebook Post: 6:53a.m. - Mekhi is making a liar out of all these doctors and nurses. They were for sure that he would pass four times already. BUT GOD! Doctors said they have done all they can do BUT GOD!! Me and dad stayed with him overnight thinking the worse would happen BUT GOD!! He still fighting! He gon' keep fighting until he can't no more. They don't really have an explanation as to why he is still here, and I keep telling them BUT GOD! They said a week ago when we got here that his intestines were all dead BUT he had two bowel movements yesterday BUT GOD!! They told me yesterday that it would be best if I pulled the plug and of course I thought about it because watching him suffer is killing me. I asked God to show me a sign and for the first time since Monday, my peanut opened his eye. BUT GOD! They said clinically he is already dead but in all my years I've never seen a dead person move their head arms and feet when you touch him, BUT GOD! I stopped believing in miracles a time ago but after seeing Mekhi make the doctors scratch their head all I can see and say is BUT GOD!! RIGHT NOW, LORD. He is helping me to turn this test into a testimony. When all is said and done, he will know that his mommy was a better advocate than any doctor or nurse.

MEKHI'S STORY

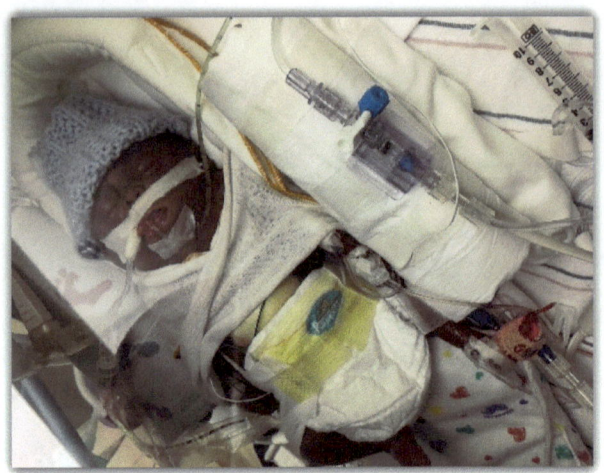

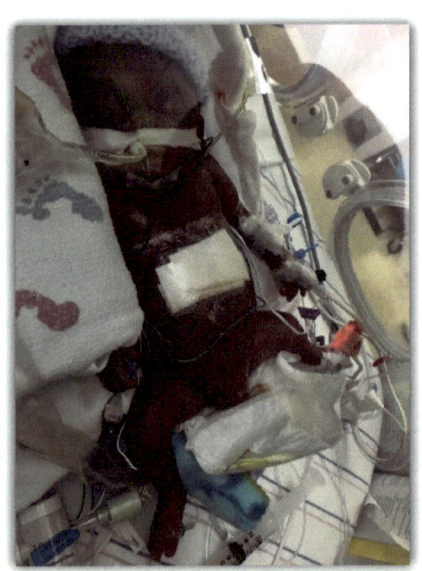

MEKHI'S STORY

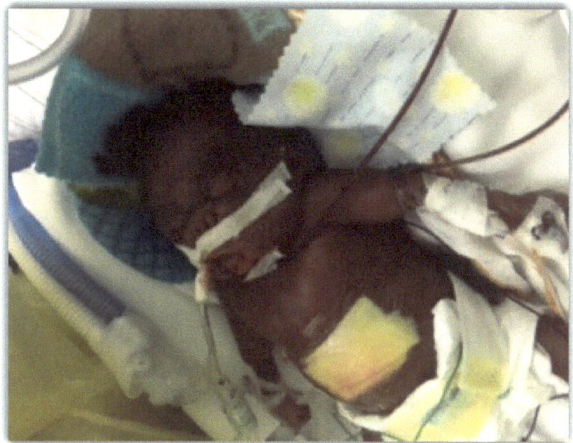

Facebook Post: 3:07p.m. - I know what it's like to be given hope and have it snatched away in the same day. Sad to say things won't turn around for my peanut, unless a miracle happens. But for right now his battle is coming to an end. Well I will just keep him close to my heart until God's will is done.

MEKHI'S STORY

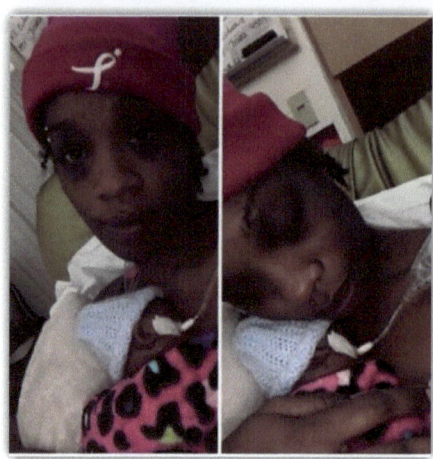 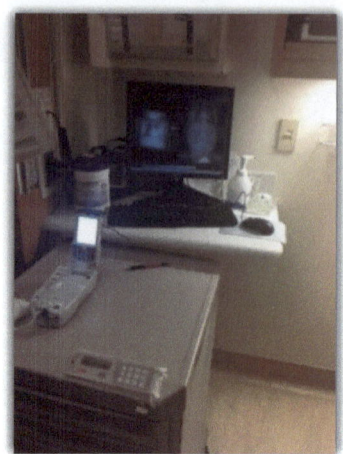

Facebook Post: 7:49 p.m.- Forgive me but I have a no man left behind frame of mind. No matter what the situation. I will drag a dead horse back to life. Only if my love was enough to keep you.

MEKHI'S STORY

October 19, 2015

CHAPTER 26

Reality Set In

Whenever my breasts would hurt, I'd always make time to pump and store my milk in anticipation that Mekhi would one day be able to drink. I pumped at home and I pumped at the hospital. Over time, my freezer at home contained nothing but breast milk and frozen chicken patties.

MEKHI'S STORY

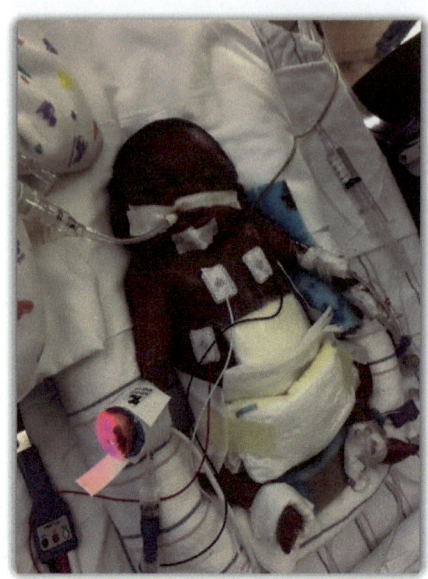

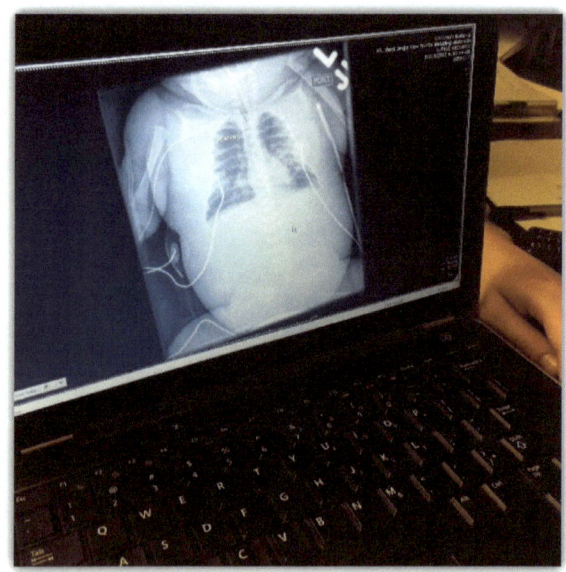

MEKHI'S STORY

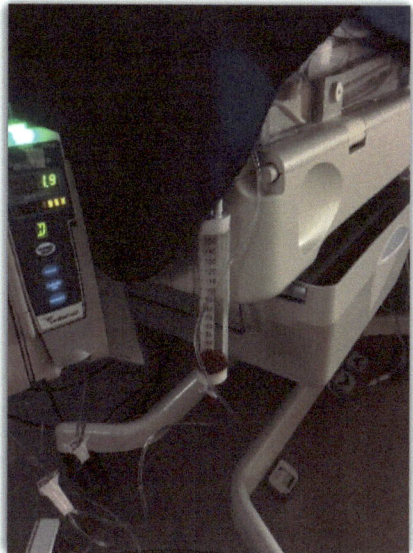

My son began urinating blood again. His organs are shutting down. Hurt is an understatement and I can't find the words to express how I am feeling. My son is dying and today it set in.

October 20, 2015

CHAPTER 27

Return to Sender

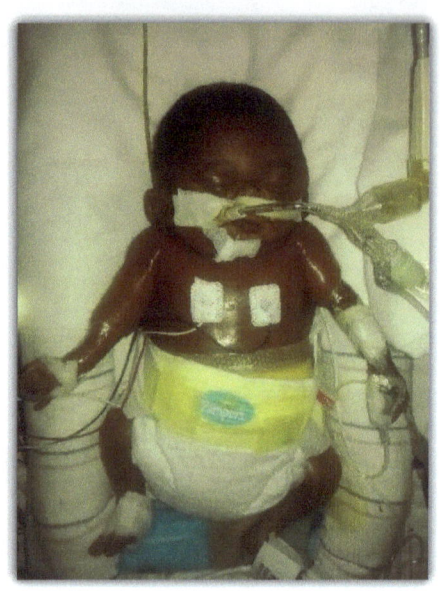

This morning was especially difficult for me. I had it in the back of my mind that if when I got to the hospital and Mekhi's fluid filled body had not went down then I would pull the plug myself. It was absolutely heart breaking and devastating to watch the fluid stretch my child's body out beyond recognition. Days prior, his body had begun to swell so bad that the fluid ripped through his skin and seeped out like running water. You don't know the suffering that I witnessed. It was like watching a crucifixion. A totally innocent baby is lying on his death bed. Completely sin free, and yet he suffered like no other. Just the sight of him was beginning to make me sick. That was my child and I loved him to death. I will say that again! That was my child and I loved him to death. Imagine if I had loved him to life.

There had better be improvement or I will have no choice but to return him to his sender. I refuse to continue watching a flower die slowly. I approached the security desk at the hospital to get my visitor's pass for the day. My face swollen, and eyes blood shot red. I don't even think I made eye contact as I handed the receptionist my identification card. Out of the corner of my teary eye, I saw a young lady stand up and reach out to hold my hand.

Facebook post: 8:29a.m. "Random word from a total stranger who seen the hurt in my eyes: There is nowhere the Lord will take you, where God's grace won't cover you."

I suppose she could feel my heart, well its heaviness. I was so angry, bitter and mad at the world that all I could do was snatch my ID card and yell out, "Oh my stars at night. What do I have? A glass forehead lady? There is no Lord, there is no God. It there was such an existence then he wouldn't let the totally innocent suffer while the wicked people of the world, prosper. Save that sermon."

It was a long walk up to the NICU. I compared it to walking "The Green Mile." I knew in the pit of my stomach that there would be no improvement. For a moment I wished those fluids had washed his body anew. This pain is unbearable. Once I got to his room, I laid my head on his incubator and

MEKHI'S STORY

closed my eyes before unveiling the baby that lied there, covered by blankets that I bought for him to go home with. My home, that was. I said a quick prayer, opened my eyes and pulled the blanket back. Sharp pains went through my chest and I fell back into a chair. What in God's green earth was that in my child's bed? He was totally unrecognizable. Fluid had ripped through his precious hands and feet, leaving skin tears everywhere. That means an infection and more skin breakdown would soon follow.

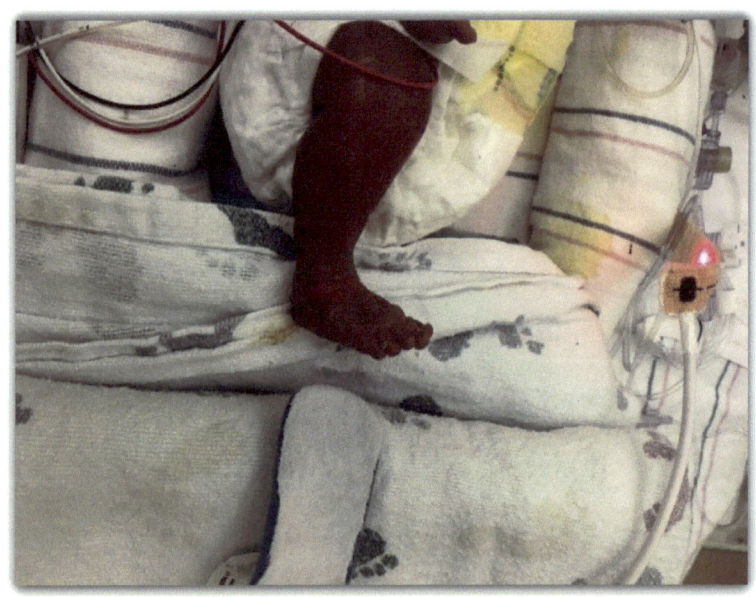

The surgical wound on his stomach had seeped a mix of blood and fluid. His precious cheeks and mouth had begun to split from the swelling in his face. The ears on my sons' head looked like they would fall off if they got any bigger. I opened his incubator to smell his neck. Even that had changed. The sweet smell of his neck had changed into a horrible stench of death. It was a sour scent from the oozing fluids and blood. "This is it", I cried! What on earth had I done to him? What are these nurses and doctors doing to my boy? What's in the medications that they are giving him? Surely nothing natural, I thought. Had I been so selfish that I put his wellbeing last? Forgive me my child. I didn't want to count him out. I wanted to believe that miracles happen. I had waited for a miracle to pass through his room for so long.

Facebook post: 2:25p.m. "You never know how much you can get through until you are going through it.

The nurses prepared Mekhi to come out of the incubator so that I could hold him. My God I was terrified. Parts of his body was smashed in and had a mangled appearance. The tape across his face looked so tight since his body was bloated. He had a forced smile on his face. I didn't want to hurt him any further and I didn't want him to die alone. He needed to know the love and remorse in my heart. Why leave me with this choice? I knew that he was suffering tremendously. You can't possibly expect me to pull the plug on my flesh and blood. I am the same person who can't let go of a dead situation or a toxic relationship. Mekhi had flat lined so many times. I knew he was tired. A part of me felt like he had been waiting on me to brave up and set him free myself. I was so selfish. Even with the odds against him, I still chose life. I've never lost anyone so close to me. I had two iguanas that died from old age. I had family members, old and young, that passed but they were sick and didn't come from me. It's a totally different experience losing what came from you. This is flesh of my flesh and blood of my blood.

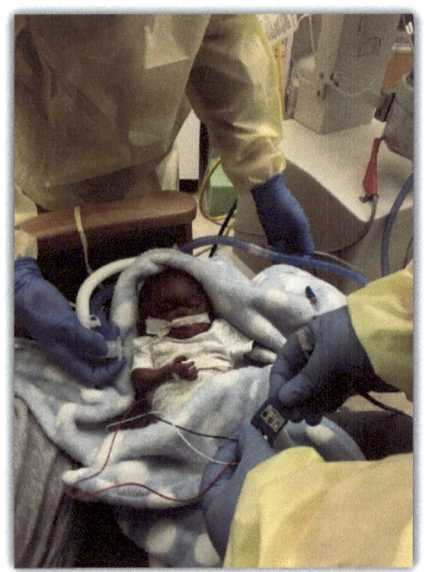

I looked down at his shiny body and whispered to him that this was it. I told him that he was the strongest soldier that I'd had the pleasure of meeting. What good is life if you cannot enjoy it? I kissed his head and made him a promise to clean my life up so that I could see him next lifetime. I let the nurses know that it was time. I had finally come to terms that my son wasn't leaving that hospital. I was finally ready to send my angel home. The nurses asked me what I wanted them to do first and I asked them to unhook everything but the ventilator and the pain medicine. It took small steps for me to let him go. All the medications were discontinued. Mekhi's father and I took turns holding him until his body went cold. I put Mekhi in the incubator to get him nice and warmed up. I had still held out hope that God would show up and show out like everyone claimed "he" does. The end was near and I could smell it. Hours had passed and his vital signs would get strong and then weak. What kind of sick game was God playing on me? Was there a waiting list to get into heaven? My son was totally sin free. He should have an expedited first-class ticket to the heavenly gates.

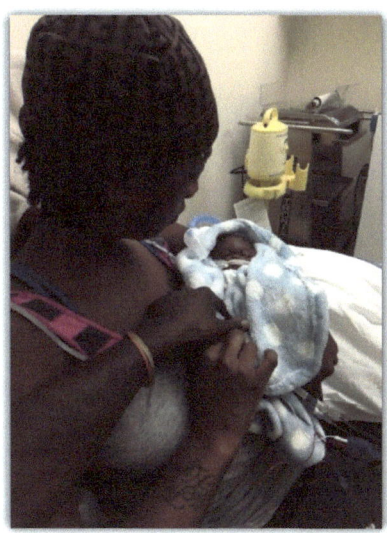

MEKHI'S STORY

My body grew cold and weak. I begged the Lord to call him home and end his suffering. The message that was meant for me to receive; I got, loud and clear. It isn't fair to make the righteous suffer. Punish me why don't you? For the first time in all my son's short life, he smiled. He lay on my chest, wrapped in a blue blanket as I moved back and forth in a rocking chair. How do you make up for lost time, I thought? I had spent much of his life trying to convince the medical team that love was all he needed. He needed his parents and his parents needed him. I lost so much time not being able to hold him that when I finally got my chance, I never wanted to let go. Mekhi knew he would be returning to his sender in due time. I'd like to think that that smile he flashed was him telling me thank you for finally choosing to see the bigger picture and put him first. I must make peace with the situation for his sake or he will continue to linger around in pure agony. I had to put my big girl pants on and let him know that his battle had been won and it was time to go home.

No easy task. By the time I looked up, we were minutes away from a new day. No improvements or miracles had passed by, or so I had thought. I was too selfish and stuck on my own level of understanding to grasp that God only takes the best. He's taking my child back to protect him. It was up to me to figure out what from. Maybe he would've had developmental delays or a painful disease that would make anyone wish for death. God only knows but I'd like to think that I have a general idea. After all the war he had gone through, he was left with a face that only a mother could love. Near impossible to recognize him and that was hurtful. Nonetheless, I loved every part of him. How could I not?

October 21, 2015

CHAPTER 28

Celebrate Death

The end is near, and it is painfully obvious. How could this little bundle of pure and absolute joy be leaving me so soon? Isn't there anything I can say or do? You truly never know how much you can get through until you are going through it. Why us God? The prayers are rolling in, but I doubt they do any good. My brother prayed a good prayer. As I rock in the rocking chair; holding tightly to Mekhi, a feeling came over me. You know the feeling, right? It's not okay now, but it will be soon and very soon. I laid Mekhi in the incubator at midnight or so. My eyes were so heavy, and I could no longer keep them open. Lord just call him home. I refuse to pull the plug on the ventilator too. I began to talk to Peanut. "Hey Guy, I promise I will be alright when you leave me. It's okay to go home; I know you are not a quitter". You truly must be "Mekhi Amir" strong to fight a battle as such. I am highly honored to have been blessed with a baby that had every reason and right to give up but did not and would not."

Do you have any idea how proud I am of him? He was the true definition of strength. It is in him that I found my strength and true calling. "Little dude, you had better believe that I will never give up. Not on you, me, your brothers and certainly not life." These eyes have witnessed a lot of pain and proud moments. The world must know that my angel existed.

MEKHI'S STORY

At one twenty a.m. I began having labor pains and contractions in my lower back. I'm talking about pain so bad that it woke me from my sleep. I jumped up and grabbed my child from the incubator he was in. the end is here! I felt it. I smelled it! Sweet mother of God, the flood gates are finally opened, and my son is being welcomed. He will be getting his wings at any moment now. I lightly tapped his father out of his sleep; letting him know to say his last words because the time had come. Hearing is the last sense to go when going through the death process. Tears flowed heavily as we watched our son gasp for his last breaths. My sweet baby was gone at one twenty-eight a.m. and no one had come to pronounce him dead until one forty a.m. Truth be told, he was born and passed at the same time. There was a message waiting to be unveiled and I would only go on to discover it after I removed myself from the hell, I put myself in.

Facebook post: 1:34A.M.

A Prayer for Family from Jonah

"Heavenly Father, please shine your light upon my family. Give us strength to overcome all the difficulties that we are dealing with now and protect us against any and all problems we may encounter in the future. O Lord, please bring us together as we are meant to be. May the love that binds us only grow stronger as we fulfill the destiny you have laid out for us.

MEKHI'S STORY

Grant my family forgiveness for any sins we have committed. May we also forgive one another Lord, as it is sometimes difficult to do.

Also, Lord in This Time in Life We Want to Focus A Special Prayer and Comfort to Chiquita Nicole Edwards And Baby Mekhi Place Your Hands and Healing on Him and Our Hearts! I Want to Say Thank You for What You've Done and Will Do!

Bless us Lord, in your name I pray,

Amen

I took to Facebook to let everyone know that I appreciated the prayers and kind words, but my soldier's battle had been won. No more suffering. My cool kid left to be with his dearly departed twin. Mekhi's dad and I are looking at our son's lifeless body in my arms; trying to figure out how to put one foot ahead of the other. I won't lie or try to minimize the numbness and bitterness that exists in my heart. My child died and parts of me died with him. Time will reveal that the part of me that died when he did, was necessary so that I may finally live. Everyone will not catch that so I will say it again. READ IT TWICE! Time would reveal that the parts of me that died when he did, was necessary so that I may finally live…. Again!

MEKHI'S STORY

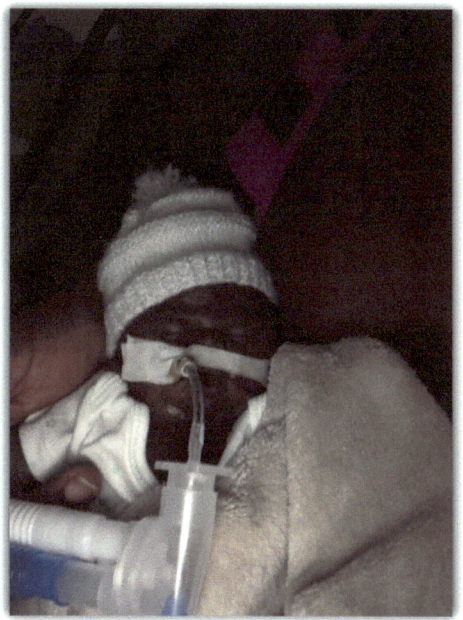

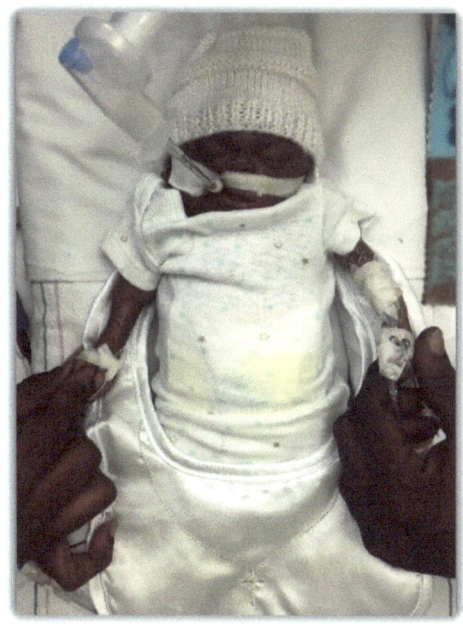

MEKHI'S STORY

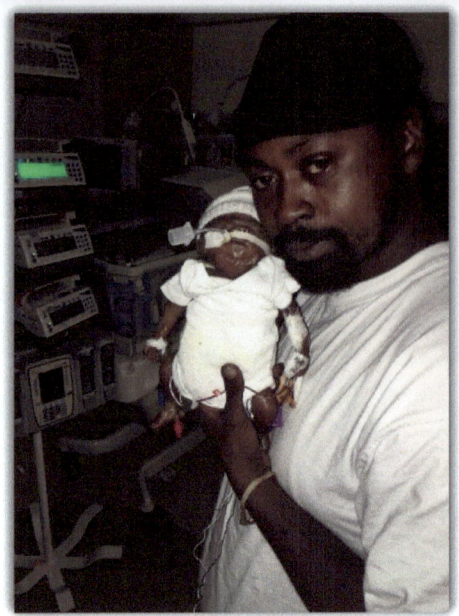

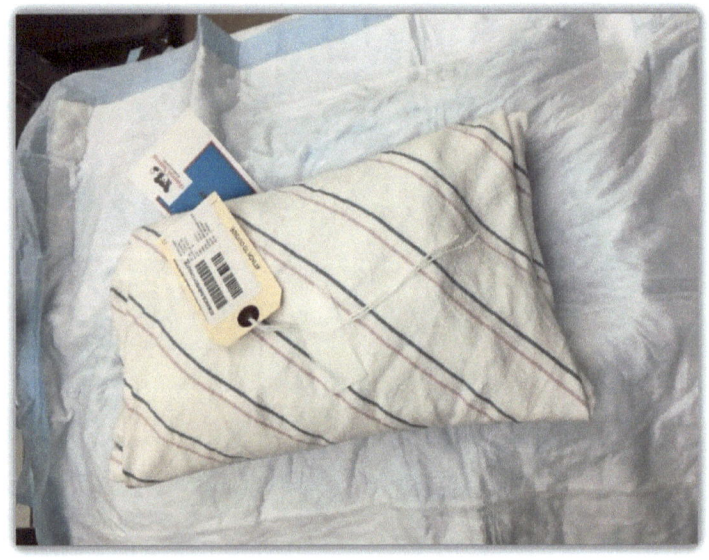

October 22, 2015

CHAPTER 29

When the Dust Settles

<u>Isaiah 57:1</u>- *The righteous perish, and no one ponders it in his heart; devout men are taken away, and no one understands that the righteous are taken away to be spared from evil. 2- Those who walk uprightly enter into peace; they find rest as they lie in death.*

Dear Mekhi,

A big part of being an unselfish parent is knowing when to let go. Knowing when to give back what was given regardless of how bad it hurts. I want you to know that I never gave up faith or hope. I fought this battle right along with you. Your time here was short but effective. You brought family together that has been estranged for years. You gave me a new meaning of life. I watched you fight until you took your last breath. I am so proud to call you my son. You have given me a reason to change my life. I want to see my angel again. To all the lives he touched, I have one thing to say, please don't let my sons' death be in vain. God called you home on October 21, 2015 at 1:28a.m. That's no coincidence. Your battle is won Peanut. No more pain and suffering in silence. Live well in the sky Mekhi. This family has met an angel and I know you are watching over us. I SAY PROUDLY, MISSION ACCOMPLISHED PEANUT! AT EASE SOLDIER!

MEKHI'S STORY

2Samuel 12:23 – He said, "While the child was still alive, I fasted and wept; for I said, 'Who knows, the Lord may be gracious to me, that the child may live.' 23- But now he has died; why should I fast? Can I bring him back again? I will go to him, but he will not return to me." (King David speaking of his infant son that died)

If you follow the teachings of the Holy Bible, you will know that Jesus Christ had literally been condemned to death for everyone's sins. He was beat and whipped beyond recognition. He suffered in silence, but with grace. They were both sin free. If there were a such thing as perfection, they'd be it. My son had to die so that I may live. Now I will ask you again.

WHO IS LIKE THE LORD?

November 14, 2016

CHAPTER 30

What Is N.E.C?

According to Children's Hospital of Los Angeles, "Necrotizing Enterocolitis (NEC) is, a devastating and excruciatingly painful disease that affects mostly the intestine of premature infants. The wall of the intestine is invaded by bacteria, which cause local infection and inflammation that can ultimately destroy the wall of the bowel (intestine). Such bowel wall destruction can lead to perforation of the intestine and spillage of stool into the infant's abdomen, which can result in an overwhelming infection and death.

Reflect to October 2, 2015, my sister recorded a video of a nurse "clearing Mekhi's lungs, even though they were already clear". The video shows him jumping in pain as she went down to far and punctured something. My guess is that she punctured his intestine. On the morning of October 3, 2015, I discovered a sausage like patty in his abdomen. The picture from chapter 10 proves that.

MEKHI'S STORY

Clinical Presentation: Abdominal distension, appearance of Sausage like patty in abdomen, swollen and or shiny abdomen, vomiting bile (green fluids), low respiratory rate, low blood pressure, low heart rate.

Necrotizing Enterocolitis usually develops within the first two weeks of life in a premature infant who is being formula fed opposed to breast milk.

Mekhi's first feeding was by way of donor milk. I had already declined the formula feeding because I know there is nothing natural about formula feeding. My only other option was donor milk since the hospital refused to give him my breast milk. Had I known that I should have questioned who the donor was I don't think his story would have went the way that it did. Immediately after the first feeding, green bile came through one of his tubes.

Diagnosis: Confirmed by presence of air bubbles in the intestinal wall on tests such as X-rays

Decreased number of platelets

Observation (gently touching the baby's stomach to check for swelling, pain and tenderness)

Treatment: Discontinue feedings

Insert orogastric tube

Administer IV fluids and Antibiotics

MEKHI'S STORY

Monitor frequently with X-rays and self-exams.

Reflect to when I said that they were ignoring my baby's pain and other symptoms. This isn't a story of me looking for someone to blame. I personally witnessed what this hospital did to Mekhi. All the hospital reports show that he only had X-rays performed once a week even after I reported obvious changes to his abdomen and overall behavior daily. I witnessed the neglect as early as September 29, 2015 and begged for his transfer. What I didn't know was that the staff knew exactly what they had did to Mekhi. They were aware of the pain they had inflicted on him. The problem is that we received Medicaid. His life was not worth saving. Looking at a financial standpoint, I made $20,000 a year, if that much. The disease he had, has been estimated to cost between $500 million to $1billion dollars to treat and an intestinal transplant would've been necessary. I wouldn't see that kind of money in 10 lifetimes they thought. I get it, it's a business. Never mind morals and integrity, right? They probably thought that I had six other children, maybe I didn't need more. Or maybe they thought that I would just have another.

They have no idea just how much Mekhi meant to me. I loss two children through Washington D.C.'s flawed system. I can't help but feel like they owe me something. They can't give back what was lost so I will settle for Mekhi's Village. Ward 8 will have a small community comprised of a shelter for pregnant women and small children, a natural birthing center, a bookstore, nail salon, restaurant, apothecary, spiritual wellness center and many other businesses. All owned and operated by my children and me. They suffered a loss just as much as I did. Our goal is to nurture and repair the indigenous community of Ward 8 by teaching self-love, self-care, cognitive behavior therapy (unlearn and relearn), in a safe and controlled atmosphere while reintroducing natural practices and holistic techniques, in order for them to be better people and essentially better parents.

MEKHI'S STORY

September 24, 2019

CHAPTER 31

Happy Birthday Peanut

I never had a funeral for my son when he died. Grief and denial kept me from having a service. Sure, I started to plan one but the thought of seeing my child's lifeless body in a casket messed my head up completely. His body was cremated and remains given to me (or so I think). You never know in the world we live in. That's another story. As the years went by, I realized that I didn't celebrate and of his birthdays. The saying goes to mourn life and celebrate death. My brother Jonah planned a birthday party for Mekhi, and I was blown away. Most of my family showed up to support me again. This was a different kind of celebration. Heartbreaking because Mekhi wasn't there physically but heartwarming at the same time.

Facebook Post: 9:51a.m. *Feeling numb*

Happy Birthday King! I miss the fighter in you, your smell, your grins and your face when you're annoyed. I still reach out for you as if you're close enough to be held. Funny how a heart can break and still beat at the same time. The hardest thing that I've ever had to hear was that my child died. The hardest thing that I've ever done is to live every day since that moment. I cannot think of anyone stronger than a mother who has lost her child and still breathes. Let this be a reminder to

MEKHI'S STORY

everyone to mend their relationships. Just remember you can't put your arms around a memory, so hug someone you love today!!! The hardest pill that I have had to swallow is that today is my Peanuts FOURTH birthday and physically he isn't here.

Happy Birthday Angel

If Roses grow in Heaven

Lord, please pick a bunch for me.

Place them in my Mekhi's arms

and tell him they're from me.

Tell him that I love him and miss him

and when he turns to smile,

place a kiss upon his cheek

and hold him for a while.

Because remembering him is easy,

I do it every day,

but there's an ache within my heart

that will never go away.

~Author Unknown~

MEKHI'S STORY

Facebook post: I've never sung a happy birthday to someone that wasn't there to hear it. Absolutely Heartbreaking! This was the first celebration for Mekhi. Happy 4th birthday baby boy. Thank you to the family that made this happen.

MEKHI'S STORY

MEKHI'S STORY

October 17, 2019

CHAPTER 32

GETOUT!

    This is a message to all my young queens in the world that is struggling with daddy issues and accepting themselves. I feel your pain and I have been where you are. Trust and believe me when I say that you are worthy of all the love you seek. Start with loving yourself and you will serve as an example as to how you want to be treated. You do not have to accept the physical and emotional abuse that comes from weak men. That's right, I said it. Those kinds of men are weak. Any man that could raise his voice at a woman and strike her down when he is enraged is a coward. Queens, their actions are a revelation of how they feel about themselves, not you. Send their ass back home to their mothers so that she may finish her job. That isn't your burden carry. I wish I had someone like me to tell me I was good enough to walk away.

    Fact of the matter is, we all are Queens and we deserve that recognition. You should not be okay with accepting nothing less than royalty because you are royalty. Never mind the history and how much you love him or how great the sex is. Protect you first. My twin's death eats at me because I wonder what if I was strong enough to not accept what was being given to me. They'd still be here. The lesson I took away from losing Mekhi was that I had been selfish to myself as well as others. I didn't know how to let go of people and things that wasn't good for me. I watched his body bloat up and fluid pour from his wounds like rain, all because I didn't know how to let go. Your story may resemble mines, but it doesn't have to end this way. It is time that we reclaim our womanhood.

Fix your crown QUEENS! You are not the abuse that these men try to inflict on you. I put up with so much abuse because that was what I grew up seeing. Every man my mother had, beat her. As a child I was led to believe that if a man doesn't beat you then he doesn't love you. I would deliberately provoke my partner just to get a reaction (Not in Mekhi's case). Now I am quick to let go of anything that doesn't serve me. This doesn't have to be your story. Use my story to empower yourself and break the cycle.

After losing Mekhi, I binged drank myself nearly to death. The pain was too great. I was living in a transitional shelter meant to help women like me. They failed me greatly. That is what sparked my interest in developing and operating my own shelter and birthing center. House of Amir is meant to serve pregnant women with a history of domestic violence. Queens! I want to help you. Everyone deserves a safe place to continue to thrive while pregnant. Mekhi's Natural Birthing Center is meant to serve women when it is time to deliver. Hospitals are no place for pregnant women of color. Especially those on Medicaid or uninsured. It determines the level of care you and your newborn will get.

MEKHI'S STORY

As soon as the babies are born in hospitals, they are taken away from their mothers and put through vigorous and useless procedures. Babies need their mothers and mothers need their babies. The mortality rate in Indigenous women and infants are higher than any other race. Let's get back to the natural order of birthing. These hospitals are just a corporation, a business that means us no good. Mekhi should be here. He died from a disease that was preventable and treatable. Necrotizing Enterocolitis is the second leading cause in premature infant death. It's an excruciatingly painful disease. All it took was effort and commitment to save my son. They didn't see a life worth saving so they left my baby covered up as he suffered in silence. Observation is all it would have taken. Listening to me, the child's mother is all it would have taken. I didn't know it then but NEC costs millions to treat. Medicaid only pays the minimum cost. Therefore, it made more sense to them to let him die in agony.

They didn't even medicate him for pain until he was transferred and by then, it was too late. If I could do it all over again, I would've never stepped foot in the hospital I delivered him at. Four years later and I still can't bear to take my children to doctor's appointment. I despise doctors and nurses. In my eyes, they're just puppets. Their strings are being pulled by someone higher up in the corporation. For the past three years, I've devoted my time and energy into natural remedies and cures. To put it bluntly. I do not have any more children to lose.

www.ingramcontent.com/pod-product-compliance
Lightning Source LLC
Chambersburg PA
CBHW042016150426
43197CB00002B/42